Taylor,

From Mike Hobbs' descriptions, you sound very much like an "aspiring leader."

I hope you enjoy the book.

Thanks for your support.

All the best,

Bob Soderquist

D1298316

START WITH
THE ANSWER

START WITH THE ANSWER

And Other Wisdom for Aspiring Leaders

BOB SEELERT

Chairman, Saatchi & Saatchi

WILEY

John Wiley & Sons, Inc.

Library of Congress Cataloging-in-Publication Data:

Seelert, Bob, 1942-
  Start with the answer : and other wisdom for aspiring leaders / Bob Seelert.
    p. cm.
  Includes index.
  ISBN 978-0-470-45032-1 (cloth)
  1. Leadership. 2. Management. I. Title.

  HD57.7.S435 2009
  658.4'092—dc22

                                                    2009004163

Printed in the United States of America.

10 9 8 7 6 5 4 3 2 1

To my wife

Sarah,

who has been with me every step of the way.

Contents

SECTION FOUR
BUSINESS OPERATIONS: LOOKING BEYOND THE OBVIOUS

SECTION SEVEN
BUILDING CULTURE THROUGH COMMUNICATIONS

SECTION EIGHT
PERSONAL STYLE AND SPIRIT

Introduction

This is a book of wisdom.

The two words *business* and *wisdom* are rarely heard together these days. This is unfortunate, not only for its reflection on companies, but more importantly because all successful executives—from the new recruit to a CEO—whether they know it or not, are on a journey of acquiring and applying wisdom in their career. Business at its best is a richly fertile ground for acquiring and enjoying the benefits of wisdom.

This book is a collection of stories about the wisdom I have gained throughout my 40-plus years in the global world of business. During this time, I have had some unique vantage points from which to acquire and deploy wisdom. I've been fortunate to have been the Chief Executive Officer of five companies in three different industries. I've built brands and businesses, been a party to two mega-mergers, and enacted numerous turnarounds. I've also served on nine Boards of Directors, including companies in the United States, the United Kingdom, and France. These situations have been supplemented by the opportunity to learn at the Aspen Institute, the Levinson Institute, and the Center for Creative Leadership.

These stories, gathered into sections representing eight aspects of personal development in business life, are universal in the experience of any executive or aspiring leader:

1. Preparation
2. Building and managing a career
3. Business strategy
4. Business operations
5. Finance and economics
6. Leadership
7. Culture and communications
8. Personal style and spirit

My collected wisdom in each of these facets of business life has not only been attained through my own experience of discovery, trial and error, testing, evaluating, and eventually adopting philosophies and strategies, but has proven to be enduring and true in four very different and challenging business environments. First, in a mature, market-dominating international consumer packaged goods company; next in a sweeping mega-merger setting; then in an intense leveraged-buyout turnaround; and finally in the revitalizing of an advertising and creative marketing behemoth.

Some of the stories and lessons I have learned are basic and fundamental, but many are radical, and all were cutting edge at the moment. And that is often the most elusive point of wisdom in business—to do the right thing, at the right time, for the right reasons. The wise executive is also radical, especially today. The wise executive is open and receptive to learning, and is committed to inner growth.

The experiences, strategies, practices, and tactics that I am sharing in *Start with the Answer* have stood the test of time, were proven in a variety of circumstances and eras, were critical to my success, and can help you in attaining yours.

If I have to pick the most fundamental lesson that brings my philosophy of management together, it is that to succeed in business—and in life—you have to know where you are going, have the courage to take the first step to get there, and constantly hone the means by which you will reach your destination. Today, too many companies are solution-obsessed and don't spend enough time up front figuring out the destination, the true answer and outcome they are aiming for. You can waste a lot of time and money implementing solutions if you don't know where you're going. So, know where you have to be. "Start with the answer" and work your way back to the solution. Only then should the hard work of crafting the solution—the vehicle for reaching the desired destination—begin.

The first time I put the "start with the answer" principle into practice was in the 1960s, when I was at Harvard Business School preparing to become a "Captain of Industry." The case studies that had the most influence on my career decisions involved General Foods Corporation—in its day, a Dow Jones Index company and one of the premier consumer packaged goods enterprises in the world. I knew that I wanted to have a career in marketing and the case studies on General Foods gave me great insights into the company and its operations (especially its cutting edge marketing programs), so it became my first choice as a place to launch a career as a marketing professional.

General Foods was a very large and sophisticated company with an aggressive recruitment policy. It skimmed the brightest MBAs from the top business schools in the country and was well known for identifying and developing their best talent for leadership within the organization. Most of my peers were shopping around for the best job offer, but I knew General Foods was the place for me and I focused my time and efforts on getting hired there.

My strategy paid off, and after earning my MBA in 1966, I embarked on a professional career in marketing and general management at General Foods. My initial job with the company was a sales internship, calling on supermarkets around Long Island, New York. I stayed on for the next 23 years, having 17 different roles and positions across the organization. Moving from sales and marketing to general management, I eventually became a senior executive and then Chief Executive of Worldwide Coffee and International Foods.

I was there in 1985 when Philip Morris acquired General Foods in what was, at the time, the largest acquisition outside of the oil industry in U.S. corporate history. This gave me insights into the dynamics of a mega-merger. As a participant in what unfolded, I observed that the process would have benefited from more "start with the answer" thinking up front to shape the overall outcome, rather than proceeding event by event, which was the tactic employed by those leading the merger and the subsequent integration activities.

I had the opportunity to apply these lessons at a later stage in my career when I led the highly successful merger of Saatchi & Saatchi with Publicis Groupe of France in 2000.

My experiences at General Foods were followed by a turnaround leadership challenge in the early 1990s at Topco Associates, a grocery industry cooperative that had become stagnant and had no competitive edge in the industry. Prior management had been consumed with increasing the efficiency of existing programs. My "start with the answer" approach in this case was to focus on revitalizing growth by attracting and increasing our client base via new product lines, refreshed packaging, and dynamic new marketing programs.

In 1991, my career entered a third phase when I was tapped as CEO to lead a leveraged-buyout turnaround situation at Kayser-Roth Corporation, a leading U.S. manufacturer of branded hosiery and leg wear based in Greensboro, North Carolina.

The company had been acquired by a joint venture of the Blackstone Group and Wasserstein-Perella and I found myself in charge of a high-intensity, hands-on, "make things happen" operation. In this case, we "started with the answer" that within three years we wanted the company to be performing at a level that would make it attractive to a strategic buyer or capable of being taken public. This required setting higher expectations supported by a vision and breadth of activities that re-energized the entire organization. Previous management had been less ambitious and focused on doing one thing at a time. The turnaround was successful, and the company was eventually sold to a strategic buyer.

In July 1995, following a series of unprecedented business events in London, I was appointed to lead the parent company of Saatchi & Saatchi—arguably the most famous name in advertising and a true worldwide ideas company.

Entering the fourth and current phase of my career, I hired Kevin Roberts, a mercurial CEO, and together we took an organization that could have fallen away, to what has become one of the most successful creative companies of this time. We "started with the answer" that we would become a high-performing creative network within the industry, growing faster than the market rate. Rather than being consumed by the problems of the past, we focused on the excitement of what could become our future. Since then, all our activities have led us towards that dream.

I consistently followed the "start with the answer" philosophy, along with the many other insights I had gained through the years—though I didn't begin to think of it as unified body of principles until 2004, when I was sitting in an executive board meeting of the Saatchi & Saatchi worldwide network in London. At that time, I had been Chairman of the company for seven years. The conversation was focused on the subject of "one-word equities"—a process by which the agency distils the essence of a brand down into a single differentiating word. At the break, I turned to Richard Myers, an Executive Creative Director at our London agency, and asked, "Richard, if I were a brand, what would be my one-word equity?" He said this was an important and interesting question, and he wanted some time to think about it. The next morning he came to me over breakfast and said, "Wisdom—that's your one-word equity."

This answer accurately reflected my current role at Saatchi & Saatchi—dispensing advice, counsel, and perspective, or what one might otherwise refer to as wisdom—but it also set me on the path to what I really wanted to share with others in business.

Start with the Answer is a collection of stories that capture the experiences and values that have enabled me to become a successful corporate leader and enjoy the journey every step of the way. I hope it can do the same for you.

Enjoy!

Bob Seelert
New Canaan, Connecticut

START WITH THE ANSWER

SECTION ONE

Preparing for a Career in Business

Go with Your Gut

I first learned to be wary of so-called expert advice in 1960 at Manchester High School in Connecticut. The lesson has stayed with me throughout my career and life.

Manchester was a nice, middle-class New England town with a population approaching 40,000. One-third of the town worked at Pratt & Whitney aircraft, one-third in the insurance industry, and one-third were local businesspeople. My high school class of 1960 was to graduate 605 students; half would go on to college, and the other half directly to work.

At the beginning of my senior year I visited the Guidance Counselor to talk about applying for college. His first question was, "What school are you thinking of applying to?" I responded, "I'm thinking of applying to Harvard." Without hesitation, he said, "That's ridiculous! Nobody from Manchester gets into Harvard. They only take private school kids. Plus, do you realize it costs twenty dollars to apply?"

I went home, and when my mother asked, "How did it go in school today?" I said, "Well, I went to the Guidance Office, and the counselor said applying to Harvard was ridiculous, plus it costs twenty bucks."

To my mother's everlasting credit, she said, "Well, we'll take a flyer on it." For those not familiar with this expression, it means, "We'll give it a try even though the odds for success are low."

As a teenager who came of age in the 1950s, I wasn't prone to questioning authority, and I probably would have followed my counselor's so-called expert advice. But my mother was wise enough to know better.

She knew that if you are going to dream big dreams, you have to be willing to take a chance.

At any rate, I went ahead and applied. I entered Harvard with the Class of 1964 and it changed the course of my life.

BOB'S WISDOM: When your instincts tell you differently from "expert advice," go with your gut.

Choosing the Right Path

My father was the President of Hartford Distributors, a Budweiser beer distributorship in Hartford and Tolland counties, Connecticut. Today, Budweiser is the clear market leader in the United States, but in my father's time, it was in a neck-and-neck horse race with Schlitz, a brand that today barely even exists.

Being a beer distributor was a tough business, but my Dad built it up from scratch. Unfortunately, he had rheumatic fever as a child which damaged his heart and ultimately led to his premature death at the age of 48. I was a junior in high school at the time, and obviously such a tragic event had a big impact on my life. It made me grow up a little quicker.

My mother, surprising many people, took over his position as President of the company. This was in an era when there were not many women in business, and those who were, didn't become presidents of beer distributorships. It was an unprecedented and bold move on my mother's part.

While in college, I worked at the company doing administrative office jobs during the summer breaks. Most of my tasks related to managing the accounts receivable books. Because I was not of legal drinking age, I was prohibited from working in the warehouse or on the trucks.

By the end of my junior year at Harvard College, my mother had spent four years in the job. She was beginning to tire of work. Plus, she was planning to remarry and move to Florida. So she came to me and said, "Bob, either you are going to take this company over, or we are going to sell it."

Budweiser controlled the franchise rights and would have to approve any buyer. Selling the business was not necessarily going to be a financial bonanza, but holding on to the distributorship would mean I had a built-in career for life. Given the growth track that Budweiser was on, keeping the business would also be highly remunerative.

I thought carefully about this situation and talked it over with my wife-to-be, Sarah. In the end, I decided that running the distributorship was not something I wanted to do. I was barely of legal drinking age and not prepared to commit myself to the beer business. Additionally, I felt that under the circumstances, I would be living in my father's shadow for the rest of my life, and I did not want to do that. I wanted to strike out on my own.

I told my mother about my decision, and we sold the business that summer. In the fall, I went back to college for my senior year, graduated the following spring, got married, applied and was accepted to Harvard Business School, and went on to build an entirely different but totally satisfying life.

BOB'S WISDOM: Choose the path that is right for you, then go for it without looking back.

What I Learned at Harvard

I entered Harvard College in 1960 with the Class of 1964. It comprised eleven hundred men from all fifty states and a number of foreign countries. Half of them came from private schools and many were from wealthy families. At Harvard, I suddenly acquired access to unlimited educational and cultural opportunities. A new world opened up for me.

During the entire four years, I never got sick, and attended every class. My children still laugh at the fact that I did not cut a single session.

A question you might ask is, "What is the most important thing you learned at college?" Well, it is the belief that no matter how smart you think you are, and no matter how much you think you know, there is always someone smarter. Someone who knows a lot more about certain things than you ever will. This revelation consistently inspired me to surround myself with the smartest and most knowledgeable people I could find.

I observed other top executives do the same later in my career when I was running Kayser-Roth. Steve Schwarzman and Bruce Wasserstein, two of the smartest thinkers in finance, were on the Board of Directors. But even those two could not have possibly known all the answers to every question, so they did not hesitate to hire people with the expertise to fill in their knowledge gaps. This is the way leaders make the total of the organization much greater than the sum of its parts, and much stronger than any individual.

Unfortunately, I also have seen the consequences when leaders surround themselves with "yes men" or people who only tell them what they think they want to hear. This creates a situation whereby the organization is no stronger than the person at the top, which can be a limiting factor indeed.

BOB'S WISDOM: There is always someone smarter than you, so know your own capabilities and limitations and surround yourself with the smartest and most capable people you can find.

Expect the Unexpected

I entered the MBA Class of 1966 at the Harvard Business School. It included 680 men and three women divided into seven sections (A–G). I was one of 97 students in section D. We attended class three times a day, six days a week, and we were expected to be ready to discuss and analyze our case study assignments in detail. It was a pretty intense experience.

My favorite class was Business Policy with Professor George von Peterffy. He had been a consultant at Arthur D. Little, and ran a "no fooling around" class. Our most accomplished and polished class member was John Stang. Many in the class had professional experience, but before coming to Harvard, John had completed a rigorous management training program at General Electric. He was smart, articulate, and given his prior experience, he had an edge on the majority of us in the class. Overall, he was a very impressive guy.

Professor von Peterffy would often start the class by waving his arm with a finger pointed toward the semicircle of students, eventually landing on someone and saying, "Mr. X, how would you like to start the class today?"

One morning, the finger pointed and landed on John Stang. "Mr. Stang, how would you like to start the class today?" von Peterffy asked. The extremely capable Mr. Stang promptly unveiled his very impressive analysis of the case.

At the next class, much to everyone's surprise, the same thing happened: "Mr. Stang, how would you like to start the class today?" This was unprecedented. No one had ever been called on twice in a row. Stang, once again, unveiled yet another impressive case analysis.

The next class—surprise of all surprises—the arm waved, the finger pointed, and for the third time it landed on John Stang, but this time with a very different result. The normally polished Mr. Stang said, "Professor von Peterffy, I am not prepared today." Von Peterffy shot back, "Mr. Stang, if this were a board meeting at General Electric, would you be prepared?" Stang replied sheepishly "Yes, Sir." Von Peterffy responded with "Then why are you not prepared for my class?"

Silence fell over the stunned throng of 97 men. The professor had made his point: you must always be prepared—there are no excuses, no exceptions.

In retrospect, I am convinced that von Peterffy planned this deliberately. He purposely selected the guy the class most respected, and called on him repeatedly until he found him unprepared. It wasn't only a lesson for the day; it was a lesson to remember for life.

BOB'S WISDOM: Expect the unexpected. Always be prepared. There are no excuses and no exceptions.

SECTION TWO
Managing Your Career

How to Choose a Career

When I applied to college, my plan was to study French and spend my junior year abroad at the Sorbonne. But at Harvard, I became exposed to subjects I'd never considered before, including economics, which I found fascinating. I set aside the idea of studying French and instead majored in economics. I particularly enjoyed labor economics and the creative tension that took place between management and the workforce, so when I applied to Harvard Business School, I considered labor relations as a field of interest.

The first year of the program followed a uniform curriculum. It was designed to expose students to all the functional areas that make up a commercial enterprise. One of these was marketing, which I fell in love with. All businesses must have a product or service to sell, and to be successful, each product must meet a consumer or customer need.

By the age of 23, I was focused on marketing as a function, product management as the entry point, and General Foods as my company of choice for employment. Ultimately, it all worked out well, but it was a long way from French, the Sorbonne, and labor relations!

In 1987, I was asked to give an address on careers in business at Hamilton College in Clinton, New York. In my address, I told the students that choosing a career should be a two-step process. First, they should make a candid assessment of their strengths and weaknesses. Then they should think carefully about what they like to do best.

I advised them to begin this process on their own, but also talk with friends, family, and counselors to get some broader perspectives. For example, if you are an adaptable, convincing sort of a person who likes interpersonal relationships and occasionally could persuade "Eskimos to buy iceboxes," then perhaps you should think about a career in sales. Or if you prefer working on your own and have an analytical and numerical bent, perhaps you should think about being an accountant. It is not that a sales career is good and accounting is bad, it is just that they are very different, and people who enjoy and perform well in one are unlikely to prosper in the other.

Once you have your self-assessment, the second step is to start thinking about companies, and pick one that highly values what you like to do and will be good at. In my view, it is best to choose a company where the function you are interested in is the essence of what the company is all about. In my case, while it was true that most companies had marketing departments, at General Foods, product management was at the heart of what the company did day-to-day, and it was the track that would put me on the road to general management.

Overall, the formula for a successful career is to put together what you have a passion for and will be good at, with a company that highly values those capabilities. By doing this, you'll greatly increase your chances of success and more importantly, you'll enjoy the work that you end up doing for a living.

As you pursue this approach, you also establish building blocks that can advance your career as circumstances change. Success in one environment will prepare you for success in another. In my own case, my ability to become a marketing professional at the onset of my career set the stage for me to focus on becoming a management professional. Acquiring such disciplines in a large, sophisticated consumer packaged goods company allowed me to translate those skills into a high-intensity, turnaround situation. Having achieved that, I was prepared for the challenge of leading the British holding company Cordiant PLC following a period of tumultuous upheaval at the global advertising agency Saatchi & Saatchi, applying all the background I learned on the client side of the table to the agency side of the business.

BOB'S WISDOM: Base your career on what you are passionate about and will be good at. Then pick a company, or create a company, that highly values those capabilities.

The Interview

I became deeply familiar with General Foods Corporation at Harvard Business School through our case studies, their on-campus activities, and my own research. It had a great reputation, it would provide me with a fantastic training ground, and it was located in White Plains, New York, which was a comfortable northeast location for my young family.

I performed well in the on-campus interview and was invited to spend a day at headquarters to participate in their formal interview process. It consisted of four separate meetings, in addition to an information-sharing lunch with a recently hired individual. I remember much of that day.

My first interview was with a Product Group Manager. He was sitting behind his desk, looking at my resume and shaking his head in a rather bewildered manner. He looked up at me and said, "I just do not see how someone like you is going to compete with someone like me." A challenging beginning! I launched into all the reasons I thought I was qualified for the job.

Following lunch, my third interview was with another Product Group Manager. He sat down, put his feet up on his desk, lit a cigar, and said, "We could spend this hour with me asking you a lot of questions, or with you asking me a lot of questions. Why don't you ask me a lot of questions?" He then leaned back, put the cigar in his mouth, and went silent.

Wow! Normally, I was prepared to ask a few questions at the end of an interview, but asking questions for an hour presented a daunting task. My mind started moving at 100 miles an hour. Half of my brain was listening to his responses, the other half racing to think of the next question as he gave his replies. Somehow, I managed to fill up the time. It must have gone all right, because they offered me a job.

After joining General Foods, I gradually became involved in recruitment. The company conducted all its interviewing with line management people. I did on-campus interviews at my alma mater, as well as interviews at headquarters in White Plains. Interviewing is a less than perfect art but I developed my own technique for doing it. I followed much the same pattern with everyone so as to develop a comparative data bank. Here is how it worked.

My first question would be, "Tell me your best success story—anything, from any time or anywhere, but the thing you are most proud of." I would listen carefully to the story and then say, "That was interesting. Others might have been in the same situation and not done nearly as well. What are the distinctive factors about you that allowed you to be so successful?" What I was trying to get at was the extent to which people had made a good self-assessment, and whether their skill set was compatible with the essential requirements of product management.

Overall, I needed to assess people's attributes, accomplishments, skills, understanding of themselves, and the extent to which they had a passion for marketing, product management, and General Foods. The underlying strength of a company is its people, and spending time to find great people is time well spent.

When you are approaching an interview, you need to prepare yourself with an in-depth understanding of your target company, the people who lead it, its industry, and why you will be a good fit in meeting their needs. Your ability to be articulate about all those factors and your own self-assessment will spell the difference between success and failure.

BOB'S WISDOM: Be ready for anything when being interviewed, and develop a plan that works for you when you are the interviewer.

Your Clothes Are Talking about You

The primary mission for the professors teaching the Harvard Business School Class of 1966 was to produce "Captains of Industry." As a reflection of the times, all the students in my class, except three women in section A, were men, and we always dressed in business suits and ties for class.

One Saturday, we arrived at our Business Policy class with Professor von Peterffy. As he usually did at the start of the class, the professor looked all around taking everything in. On this particular day, his eyes fixed on the gentleman sitting next to me, and he asked, somewhat incredulously, "Mr. Simmons is that a sports jacket you are wearing?" Simmons replied, "Yes, Sir." Von Peterffy continued, "Mr. Simmons, if this were a board meeting at General Motors, would you be wearing a sports jacket?" Simmons acknowledged, "No, Sir, I would not." This answer was followed by a query from the Professor, "Then why are you wearing a sports jacket in my class?"

Times have changed, and corporate dress codes certainly have changed. Many successful companies have no dress codes at all, and many accomplished individuals have their own distinctive marks of sartorial style.

However, whether you are just getting started or actively seeking to advance your career in business, you can expect to be judged on your appearance. As a general rule, it makes sense to dress and groom for your industry, for your department, and for the occasion. Within this context, you can cultivate a personal style that is distinctive and memorable. When in doubt, err on the side of formality.

BOB'S WISDOM: Your clothes express a great deal about you, so think carefully about your personal style and appearance. Always look sharp.

Sales Fundamentals

I started work at General Foods the Monday following graduation from Harvard Business School. Someone once asked me, "Why didn't you take some time off?" The answer was simple—at the time, I had no money and a wife and child to provide for.

I was hired into the Post Cereal Division as a Product Assistant. At that time, all newly hired marketers were required to start their career with a six-month sales internship calling on grocery stores. The idea was to learn firsthand about the retail sales environment and distribution logistics as a prelude to moving to headquarters to develop brand-marketing plans.

Assigned to the New York sales district with a route encompassing 115 supermarkets in Nassau County, Long Island, I spent my first day with a sales supervisor whose stated goal was to teach me how to "plan my work, and work my plan." He told me that I was expected to preplan my sales route and objectives and to make eight retail calls per day. The routes were planned based on targeted contact frequency and efficient drive time. Sales objectives were preset, based on the known condition of the store and the promotional calendar for products issued by headquarters.

I learned on Day One that it is the responsibility of a retail salesperson in the consumer goods industry to focus on four distinct activities: distribution, shelving, pricing, and merchandising.

Distribution is the key starting point for any product. To make a sale, the product has to be in the store. I quickly learned that the tricky part of managing this activity was that General Foods always seemed to offer many more items than the retailer had room for in the store. So, the key to successful distribution lies in establishing priorities for which products are most important to have on the shelf, in both the right sizes and the proper case packs.

The aim of shelving is to have products prominently displayed and available in quantities that eliminate out-of-stocks. Fast-moving products that required higher levels of inventory in the store occupied the lower shelves. General Foods had "Plan-O-Grams" based on sound research showing the shelving pattern that optimized sales for specific products in each section of the store.

Pricing meant ensuring that all products were marked according to the "suggested retail price" and properly aligned versus competition.

Merchandising consisted primarily of getting displays up in the stores, as well as securing print advertisements and feature prices in line with the promotional calendar.

Discharging these responsibilities also required oversight of the volume relationship with the retailer, including attention to details regarding product codes, order quantities, ship dates, and anything pertaining to the logistics of having their orders filled completely and on time.

On Day Two, I accompanied my supervisor as he made some retail calls. By Day Three, I was on my own. Thrown to the wolves!

I arrived at my first store at 8 AM, introduced myself to the store manager as "the new man from Post," and gained his agreement to check our stocks. That morning I embarked on what had to be the most thorough retail call in history. I checked every item, rotated every product for freshness, unpacked several cases of merchandise from the stockroom, corrected a variety of pricing errors, and picked up our damaged merchandise from the backroom. My final act was to make my presentation to the manager on two preset objectives: gaining distribution for a second size of a cereal brand (turned down due to lack of space), and arranging for a shipper display pack for one of our beverages (agreed and ordered for my visit the following week).

At that point, I headed out to my company car with a feeling of satisfaction until I looked at my watch. It was now 10:15 AM. I had spent two hours and fifteen minutes on this one call and still had seven more to make! At that rate, I was headed for more than a sixteen-hour workday! Another quickly learned lesson: you can't do everything on a single retail call. Rather, you must learn to set priorities and figure out what can wait until the next visit.

Four years later, I served a 12-month stint as District Sales Manager in Washington, D.C. as part of a managerial broadening experience. Subsequent to that assignment, I had the opportunity to oversee a National Sales Force as a Division Manager. What I learned then, and still know 40 years later, is that the fundamental responsibilities of a salesperson in the consumer goods industry are the same as those my Sales Supervisor taught me about on Day One. Electronic reporting may have replaced paper, but the principles of selling are all the same.

BOB'S WISDOM: Sales fundamentals in consumer goods are consistent and timeless. Keep the focus on distribution, shelving, pricing, and merchandising as you plan your work and work your plan.

Every Memo Is an Ad about You

In 1967, following the six-month sales internship with General Foods, I went to the White Plains headquarters to begin my career in product management. I was assigned to START Instant Breakfast Drink, an alternative to frozen orange juice.

My first memo to go up the line was an analysis of the latest test market results based on Nielsen panel data. It came back to me marked up in red ink with numerous comments, corrections, and suggestions such as "make it shorter, and be crisper." I had been to Harvard, but this looked like my first essay from fifth grade!

I went into my boss's office, rather red-faced and embarrassed, to chat with him about it. He said, "Bob, I know you're a bright guy, and I really want you in my group. But you need to realize that every memo that goes out over your signature is an ad about yourself. People receive it and they may or may not know who you are, but they take it as an indication of how you think and how smart you are—or are not. It forms an impression in their minds. So, from today, I want everything that goes out over your name to be as perfect as it can be and serve as an example of how you want people to think about you." Since that day, I have tried not to send out any communications that fail to meet that test.

Today, e-mails are a particular challenge. Often, under the guise of speediness, the sender fractures the English language and leaves an impression of less than complete thinking behind the message. E-mail writers beware! I often see e-mail that makes me question the care, thoroughness, or general intelligence of the writer. If that's what I think, maybe others do, too.

BOB'S WISDOM: Every communication that goes out over your name forms a lasting impression. Make it the best it can be.

Get to Know Yourself Better

In 1982, at the age of 39, I attended a two-week seminar at the Aspen Institute in Aspen, Colorado, with a group of twenty peers from across the United States, United Kingdom, Switzerland, and Canada, representing various sector backgrounds including municipal and federal government agencies, large corporations (manufacturing, media, energy, management consulting, telecommunications), and higher education. The seminar was based on the assumption that leaders, whether established or on their way up, can derive significant benefit for themselves and their companies from a systemic examination of their personal values and their place in the world. This experience had a significant impact on my life in general, and on my career in particular.

To prepare for the seminar, the attendees were expected to read excerpts from some of the greatest Western and Eastern writers and thinkers of all time, including Plato, John Milton, John Locke, Alexis de Tocqueville, Dostoyevsky, T.S. Eliot, and Martin Luther King, Jr.

We would get together on a daily basis with a moderator to debate the fundamental principles, values, and beliefs these great writers and thinkers had expressed. The objective was to help us, as individuals, to define who we were, what we believed in, and what we stood for.

One day we discussed the writings of two Chinese philosophers—Mencius and Hsün Tzu. On the one hand, the Mencius treatise, *Human Nature*, espoused the notion that humans were inherently good. The Hsün Tzu work, on the other hand, was entitled *Man's Nature Is Evil*, and he argued that humans were inherently bad. So the discussion focused on the question, "Are people inherently good or inherently bad?"

I was stunned to hear how such fundamental propositions could produce responses so varied. Even more surprising was the realization that our response to this question reflected and was consistent with virtually all our attitudes and dealings with other people in the workplace. Those who thought people were inherently good delegated responsibility and trusted their staff to act in the best interests of the company. Those who thought people were inherently bad attributed importance to things like using time clocks and checking up on employees.

Following the seminar, I wrote a Personal Statement that committed to paper who I was and what I believed in. This was a useful process that codified my own credo. Here is what it said.

Bob Seelert's
Personal Statement

I stand before you as what I would call a totally honest, open, and common sense-based individual.

A person who is an eternal optimist, and one who believes that most things in business are possible given the right people, the right attitudes, and agreement on what we want to get done.

A person who is oriented to the long term, to growth, to multifunctional teamwork, and to constant improvement in everything we do.

A person who is competitive versus the outside world, has a passion for excellence in execution, and takes pride in the performance of his organization.

A person who recognizes that one cannot get the job done alone and therefore believes in communication, delegation, and clearly assigning accountabilities.

A person who expects commitment and hard work measured against high standards, and recognizes and rewards people accordingly.

And finally, a person who has fun while he works, and who keeps work in balance with his personal life.

You may or may not agree with my personal statement, but you'll certainly benefit by writing your own.

BOB'S WISDOM: Find the best avenue for getting to know yourself better and write a personal statement identifying the values, beliefs, and principles you stand for. Then live by it.

I'm an ENTJ, What Are You?

In June 1993, I took my Kayser-Roth management staff to the Center for Creative Leadership in Greensboro, North Carolina, for a team-building session. Part of our agenda included taking the Myers-Briggs Type Indicator test. This is a tool that provides a useful measure of personality by looking at eight preferences that all people use at different times, and organizing them into four scales. People (and their organizations) use this test to better understand themselves and their practices, heighten their appreciation of others, and make constructive use of individual differences. The validity of the test is well documented in studies conducted over more than 50 years.

The test categorizes people into 16 different types. I came out as an ENTJ (Extravert, iNtuitive, Thinking, Judging). The descriptive words for this type are logical, decisive, tough, strategic, critical, controlled, challenging, straightforward, objective, fair, and theoretical. The dominant function for an ENTJ is Thinking, and the auxiliary function is Intuition. ENTJ's have a lot of "CEO-like" qualities, but they also need to ensure they factor in the human element, appreciate the contributions of others, check the quality of their resources before going forward, take time to reflect and consider all sides, and learn to identify and value feelings.

I thought my results accurately described who I am, and I considered the less than positive traits the results revealed about me to be valid and useful. Overall, the test helped me to positively understand myself and importantly, to further develop my abilities.

I also learned the personality types of my staff, and gained a much better understanding of how to complement and deploy them most effectively. Prior to these team-building sessions, there had been times when the behavior of various people puzzled and frustrated me. Now I felt that I understood the underlying reasons for them, which enabled me to take better advantage of their diverse capabilities.

When I became Chief Executive at Cordiant, awareness of my own personality profile was a definite advantage and helped me to anticipate and manage the more creative Myers-Briggs profiles of the people I needed to relate to there. It got me off to a faster start with fewer frustrations.

BOB'S WISDOM: Knowing your Myers-Briggs type leads to understanding yourself. Knowing those of your staff helps you to better utilize their capabilities.

You Learn More from Failure than from Success

In January 1967, my first General Foods assignment in product management was START Instant Breakfast Drink six weeks before it was to be introduced nationally. Little did I know that it was about to become the largest disaster in the history of the company to date!

START was an orange-flavored powdered breakfast drink. It came in an easy-to-open canister and was mixed with water to make a reconstituted beverage. It was similar to TANG, the drink that went with the astronauts to the moon, but START had a more adult taste profile and was made in quart-size batches instead of by the glass. The competitive frame was frozen orange juice. START tasted great, had more vitamin C than orange juice, and was more convenient. It had two years of test marketing behind it, and projections indicated that it would be about twice the size of the TANG business. All in all, it was a very attractive investment.

I can still remember being handed the introductory marketing plan. It was in a three-inch thick binder and incredibly impressive. The advertising proclaimed, "The Trouble with START is to Stop" and the spending plan included a massive budget for its day. The promotion plan was to mail full-size canister samples to 20 million households nationwide. All the elements of the plan had been carefully proven in test marketing. Management was convinced that START would be a surefire success.

There was just one big problem. That year, the Florida orange growers were harvesting what turned out to be the most bountiful crop of oranges in history. A huge oversupply meant a plunging price for frozen orange juice, with promotional prices reaching 10 cans for a dollar (compared with START at 29 cents per canister).

The thick, impressive marketing plan with all the test market results had never tracked the fact that throughout the entire test marketing process START had been more economical per serving than frozen orange juice. Suddenly, it would be much more expensive than the real thing. The laws of economics took over and plunged the whole undertaking to an untenably low sales level. Yes, START tasted great, and yes, it had more vitamin C, and yes, it was more convenient. But all the ads and samples in the world could not reverse the fact that consumers were now being asked to pay significantly more for a replacement product than for the real thing.

The reality was that sales came in at 50% of budget, the introduction lost considerable money, and START failed to survive.

For me, however, it was a great experience. Rather than ride the coattails of somebody else's success, I was part of the group that had to rethink and redo every element of the marketing plan in the context of the sobering consumer-focused reality thrust upon us. I ended up learning more than I ever could have in a stable, onward and upward environment.

Most of all, I learned to truly respect the consumer, to dig for the real facts, and to make sure that I could see the big picture.

BOB'S WISDOM: You learn most from failure; more than you can from success.

How to Become a Senior Executive

When I started my career at General Foods, my ultimate goal was advancing to general management. I was sure that it would be a great training ground, and I also knew that at General Foods, product management was the road to general management.

I spent 23 years there basically because every time I was ready to take on a new challenge, the company had a new job to offer me. I had 17 different jobs in that time span. I spent 12 years in marketing and sales, three years as a division manager, and eight years as a multidivisional executive.

During my 12 years in marketing and sales, I had 13 different assignments. The shortest was for six months, and the longest was for 20 months. This implies greater discontinuity than there actually was, because some of the assignment changes graduated to greater responsibilities within the same business category. Nevertheless, it is true that there is a high level of turnover in assignments and people in product management.

Many observers would argue that there is too much. But there is a reason this turnover is desirable and necessary. It is natural and expected that creativity, in most circumstances, has an inevitable arc; at some point even the best minds will run out of drive and fresh ideas. In my experience, high-powered people tended to come into a new assignment with a clean slate. They would immediately devour everything they possibly could about the brand involved and offer new perspectives and new ideas, thereby, contributing to the brand's market success. But, after a certain period, let's say three years, they would run out of fresh ideas. When that happened, it was time for that individual to move on and for a different face with new ideas to take over.

Product management does indeed prepare one for positions in general management. While it is "responsibility without authority," it integrates marketing, sales, operations, research, human resources, and finance from a brand point of view. It is also a great training ground for the disciplines of planning and dealing with external resources.

I ultimately became a general manager. However, the most challenging and productive phase of my career occurred three years later when I became a Group Vice-President responsible for multiple divisions. It is one thing to be the hands-on, responsible person for a brand, category, or division. It is something else to be directing multiple divisions, each led by a hard-charging individual.

This is the stage where leadership takes over from management, and inspiration and coaching begin to play significant roles. Your intimate knowledge of a business no longer gets it done for you. Rather, it is your ability to unveil fundamental values, beliefs, and principles that can inspire others, transcend particular businesses, and produce good results all at the same time. If you are successful at this stage, then you'll be a candidate for the job of Chief Executive Officer.

BOB'S WISDOM: Your pathway to general management and positions of leadership requires that you demonstrate success in a great number of increasingly responsible roles, while consistently inspiring others through your values, beliefs, and principles.

The Importance of a Great Executive Assistant

Having a great executive assistant will be a key component to your success, so you had better find the right one. The question is, "What are the key attributes you should look for in the person you select?"

I have been blessed with a succession of excellent professionals: Winnie Woodhull and Joan Hamshire (General Foods), Peggy Conley (Topco), Judy Cummings (Kayser-Roth), followed by Alison Bromhead, Dorothy Musche, and Trudy Vitti (Cordiant and Saatchi & Saatchi). The following are the attributes they shared that I found to be of particular importance.

First, executive assistants have to realize and accept that their first responsibility is to do everything they can to help you achieve your objectives. As key support professionals, their role is to make you a "better you" by anticipating, processing, and executing the details of your daily life.

This is important for you, but it is also enlightened self-interest for them. Like it or not, the careers of executive assistants are often tied to the success of their boss. If you are successful, your executive assistant will usually prosper. If you fall by the wayside, your assistant may have to start over as well.

On the job, the key watchwords for your executive assistant are "flawless execution." The successful businessperson leads a very busy life. It is essential that all day-to-day activities go according to plan to the greatest degree possible. Making sure that you are in the right place, at the right time, and fully prepared to conduct the business of the moment is your executive assistant's job. They must organize and execute this to be 100% accurate and on time.

Executive Assistants are an extension of your office. How they answer the phone, greet people, and deal with your clients and associates, as well as your subordinates, is a reflection on you. If they are harsh and abrasive, people will attribute that to you, not just to them. In this regard, call your own number every once in a while to get a sense of their telephone manner. I hope it will be as pleasing as yours would be if you were answering the phone yourself.

Along the same line, never permit your executive assistant to "talk down" the company. Again, this would be a reflection on you.

The days when executives had a secretary to do basic typing, filing, and managing appointments, are far behind us. Today's executives need assistants who are technologically savvy, capable of learning new and improved programs for word processing, managing data, producing written and numerical reports, and conducting online research. Of course, it is still the case that your executive assistant can give a dramatic boost to your productivity by handling correspondence and effectively taking dictation. I can remember Winnie Woodhull patiently spending hours with me as I was learning how to dictate memoranda.

Executive assistants must maintain confidentiality and be discrete. Inevitably, they will become aware of sensitive matters and private discussions that must remain exactly that.

They must know where you are and be able to reach you at all times. At a moment of crisis, this will be of the utmost importance.

Your executive assistant should meet with your personal accountant and ensure that your record keeping is impeccable from a tax return point of view. Being able to document and prove where you are every hour of every day can be invaluable if you ever face a tax audit.

Finally, if you are in New York City and you are a chief executive, try to get your executive assistant invited to join the Seraphic Society.

This is an organization of people who work with chief executives, and it is fabulous for networking. Dorothy Musche and Trudy Vitti are both members.

BOB'S WISDOM: Hiring an executive assistant who is well qualified, experienced, and importantly, can identify with and support your success, is a key ingredient in building your career.

You'll Need to "Work Your Ass Off"

By the time he addressed our team at General Foods, Jack Twyman had strung together three careers, each impressive in its own right. He had been a Hall of Fame basketball player in the National Basketball Association; a successful sportscaster on the NBA Game of the Week for ABC television; and finally, Chairman and CEO of Super Foods Services, Inc., a major food distributor in the United States. A man with three consecutive career successes surely would have some important advice for us, and he did.

The most significant lesson we learned from Jack was the importance of hard work, preparation, and dedication. From early in his life, he felt anything was possible, as long as the person was willing to pay "the price." The definition of the price is an absolute and total commitment to what you want to accomplish.

Jack went to Central Catholic High School in Pittsburgh, Pennsylvania, where basketball was a highly competitive sport. He tried out for the team as a freshman, sophomore, and a junior, and was cut each time. During the summer between his junior and senior years, he wore out three pairs of sneakers practicing basketball on the playground. As a senior, he made the team, went on to play at the University of Cincinnati and the NBA, and ultimately was inducted into the Basketball Hall of Fame. What an incredible record of achievement and testimony to personal commitment, preparation, drive, and energy.

Jack's selection by ABC as Game of the Week announcer was not happenstance, but a result of his thorough preparation for the job. For Jack, there was never any magic formula for success. Rather, as he said, "I worked my ass off!"

BOB'S WISDOM: There is no substitute for dedication and hard work.

Stay in Touch with Recruiters

After Kayser-Roth was sold to a strategic buyer at the beginning of 1994, I had to figure out the next steps in my career.

I spent the following year trying to acquire the Tetley worldwide tea and coffee assets from Allied Domecq, an international company with headquarters in Bristol, England. I lined up financial support from Citicorp Venture Capital, and built a team of supporting executives drawn from my days at General Foods. We developed a business plan, and I even had a list of eight things we were going to do the first week we took over the company. The only problem was that we finished second in the bidding process! When you are trying to acquire a company, second is the same as one millionth—you do not get the company.

The final bidding took place in London. While I was there, the print and broadcast media were buzzing about a row at Saatchi & Saatchi PLC between the company's investors and the founding brothers. Ultimately, the brothers departed and opened a new, competitive agency. Various clients left the original company, and the whole place seemed to be in chaos. The company renamed itself Cordiant to eliminate confusion between the holding company's activities and those of its networks. I thought to myself, "What a wild situation."

Shortly after I returned to the United States I was called by an executive recruiter from Spencer Stuart, the leading privately held global executive search firm who, lo and behold, wanted to talk with me about my potential interest in taking the job as Chief Executive at Cordiant!

Over the years, I had maintained a relationship with executive recruiters, in particular with the Spencer Stuart people, as they had placed me at Kayser-Roth. It is good practice to maintain a relationship with executive recruiters because to a great extent you have to expect to manage your own career. Today, there are not many companies left that actually do that for you.

Spencer Stuart played a significant role in drawing up the spec for the Chief Executive role at Cordiant. It had four components. First, the individual had to appreciate the role and importance of advertising, but did not have to be an "ad person." In fact, given the situation, the person had to have a broad range of business skills. Second, it had to be someone who had run an international business. This was a multicultural company with offices all over the world. Third, it should be someone who had been successful in turnaround situations. This was a company in chaos, and it needed someone who would be unflappable in those circumstances. Finally, the company historically had not been very successful in the United States, and they wanted someone who understood U.S. clients—perhaps even an American for a British-based publicly listed company.

It was this spec that led them to call me. I had spent more than $2 billion in advertising on more than 60 different brands through seven different advertising agencies. I had run an international business as President and CEO of General Foods Worldwide Coffee and International Foods. I had directed the successful turnarounds at Topco and Kayser-Roth, and I understood the U.S. market.

I met with representatives from Spencer Stuart, people from Cordiant, and members of their Board. I then asked permission to talk with two advisors. The first was a consultant I had worked with and who knew me very well. He said, "Don't touch this with a ten foot pole." He thought the company was beyond repair, and he was mindful that there was a poor track record for people moving from the client side to the agency side of the consumer goods industry.

I moved on to my second advisor, the former head of an advertising agency. He thought taking the job was a great idea. He felt the Spencer

Stuart spec was the right formula for the situation, and he remarked, "These kinds of businesses are hard to kill. Clients don't want to disrupt strategic relationships. They want stability."

I went home to sort out my decision. I thought the job would be something new, different, interesting, and challenging. From an economic point of view, I thought it fitted the theory of the low base—the stock price had sunk about as low as it could get, so I figured there had to be a significant upside. The idea of living in London appealed to my wife and me, as our children were all grown up. Overall, I thought it would be a bit of a hoot!

We decided to take the job. It was an adventure in life, and it all worked out very well. Cordiant subsequently demerged Saatchi & Saatchi, and I am writing this book 14 years later as the nonexecutive Chairman of the company where I provide advice, counsel, and perspective.

BOB'S WISDOM: Proactively manage your own career. Maintain relationships with executive recruiters, get good advice, and then go with your heart.

SECTION THREE
Planning and Other Essentials of Business Strategy

Start with the Answer

My most important management philosophy is "Start with the answer, and work your way back to the solution." As a starting point, I apply this approach to virtually every situation that comes across my desk. Once you understand the basic facts, where you want to position your organization or yourself should become obvious. The real question is, "How do you get there?" Instead of wasting time dwelling on the problems of the past, you should devote all your energy to creating solutions for the future.

Such was the case when I checked in at Cordiant in July 1995. At the time, the company was losing money due to the tumultuous events of the previous six months. The founders of the company were gone, 6% of the revenue had walked out the door with them, and a large amount of debt was coming due far too soon. Not a pretty picture!

The first two priorities were stabilizing clients and staff, and refinancing the company. Many of the people in the company were caught up in the issues of the day and all the reasons we were losing money. To refinance the company, we needed to produce a credible five-year financial forecast.

Rather than responding to gloomy forecasts, we chose a totally different approach. We started in the external world of the industry in which we were competing by assessing how the Peer Group Composite, made up of Omnicom, WPP, and Interpublic, was performing. After all, these companies were in the same business we were in, we competed for new business in the same pitches, and the market dynamics that affected them were the same ones that affected us.

We learned that we were in a growth industry with worldwide media spending increasing at a rate of 5–7% per year. Beyond that, the major holding companies were growing at a faster rate due to trends toward globalization and clients consolidating advertising resources. The Peer Group Composite was achieving operating income in the range of 10–12% of revenue. Adjusting our business for the scale effect of their larger businesses, we concluded that if 10–12% margins were attainable by them, then an 8–10% range ought to be achievable by us. These business parameters became "the answer," and we could now devote all our energies to doing what it would take to get us there.

Recognizing the dire nature of our starting point, we set a three-year time frame for success. Three years later we were there, having grown revenues faster than the market rate and earnings per share better than 25% per year. The key element in this achievement was starting with where we wanted to get to, rather than being consumed by the depths of the situation we were in.

BOB'S WISDOM: The first step in a business plan is to "start with the answer" and then devote all your time and energy to work your way back to the solution.

How to Do Strategic Planning

A t Harvard Business School, the entire curriculum was taught by the case method, each one distilling a real-world situation. We were provided with facts and figures and asked to respond from a chief executive's perspective, "What would you do if you were Mr. X at the ABC Company?" Each night, I prepared three cases, and the next day I was ready to present and defend my point of view in a discussion with 96 of my peers.

The thing that constantly amazed me about these case study discussions was how 97 people could look at the same data and come to entirely different conclusions on how to proceed.

So it is with strategic planning. Accordingly, you have to approach strategic planning with a clearly defined point of view.

My point of view is that of an eternal optimist. I believe that almost anything in business is possible given the right people, the right attitudes, and the right resources. The first two commitments I want my organization to make are to growth and constant improvement in everything we do. This sets a tone for developing and cultivating great ideas needed to move the business ahead, and ensures that the organization's efforts are oriented to "onward and upward."

Sometimes you have to shake things up or change the playing field to pursue this point of view legitimately. As an example, let's take the coffee business at General Foods in the 1980s. As an indicator of the scope of our worldwide business at that time, coffee was the second largest commodity in world trade, next to oil.

If we defined the playing field as U.S. grocery retail coffee purchased for consumption at home, then the market was modestly declining, the company already had a high share, and competition was intense from other national brands and regional roasters.

Conversely, if we defined the playing field as the world, and coffee consumed out of home as well as at home, then we had an entirely different picture. The market was growing instead of declining, there were multiple acquisition opportunities, and the out-of-home market presented exciting possibilities, including equipment innovations. There were even parts of the world like China, where coffee was emerging as a new beverage of choice, especially for young people eager to embrace Western culture.

To crystallize and take advantage of these opportunities, General Foods restructured and reoriented its coffee business toward production, marketing, and distribution on a worldwide basis. This required strategic planning that transcended regional boundaries and embraced a wider view of the world as our playing field.

BOB'S WISDOM: Strategic planning is a state of mind, and your point of view determines the outcomes. Growth and continuous improvement are your benchmarks.

Ten Rules for Leading the Turnaround of a Declining Business

I have been involved in turnaround situations at Topco Associates, Kayser-Roth Corporation, and Cordiant. The similarities between these situations were greater than the differences.

In each case, they were companies that had fallen on hard times, but there was a belief that they could rise again like a phoenix from the ashes. Additionally, the fact that the companies were not doing well was by no means a secret to the employees, who were always eager to have the leadership that could bring it all back together and get things moving again.

Here are my ten rules for a successful turnaround:

Rule 1. When formulating goals, start with the answer and work your way back to the solution. Do not get bogged down in the morass of yesterday. Get going toward where you need to be in the immediate future. At Cordiant, we developed a five-year financial forecast within three months of arrival that we used as the basis for refinancing the company. Subsequently, we exceeded every benchmark of that forecast.

Rule 2. Get out in front of people immediately and position yourself as the new leader in the company. Tell them who you are, what you believe in, why you are there, your perspective on the situation, and how you intend to proceed. At Cordiant, I visited all the principal people and major locations in London and New York in my first two days.

Rule 3. Bring an extraordinarily high sense of urgency to what you are doing, but also look before you leap. People are anxious for results, but this is no time for dead ends. Think carefully about everything you do, but keep moving. At Topco, we immediately commenced development of a line of environmentally-friendly products because there was an obvious niche and need in the market for them.

Rule 4. Do not sit around headquarters! Get out to where the work is done—plants and field offices. You need this input, and you need to be a motivating force for people. At Cordiant, I got around to offices accounting for 60% of our revenues in the first six months.

Rule 5. Go out and listen to customers and clients. At Kayser-Roth, one of my first visits was to Wal-Mart. They told me, "Mr. Seelert, we are concerned about the viability of your company as a supplier." Two years later, we were named their vendor partner of the quarter. If I had not personally gone there to listen and learn, I doubt that this would have happened.

Rule 6. Listen to everybody in the organization who offers an opinion about the business—don't just hang around with the people who report to you. There are two sides to all coins and stories. You need to understand both. If you can, meet with your competitors or the heads of similar organizations. When I went to Cordiant, I met with the heads of other holding companies, agency networks, consultancies, and service organizations.

Rule 7. Recognize that you cannot get the job done alone. Open communications and clearly assigned accountabilities are essential. Your visits to locations provide the forums for rallying and directing the teams, as well as quickly identifying the true talents across the organization.

Rule 8. Lay out your vision, purpose, values, beliefs, objectives, strategies, and plans for accomplishment as quickly as possible. People cannot really get going until you set the right direction. At Cordiant, I laid out my initial vision on day one: to be the "World's Best Creative Communications Resource." I indicated that I would be a good listener and that together, we would drive the vision forward from there.

Rule 9. If you do not have the internal resources to get the jobs at hand done, do not be afraid to use outside resources. At Cordiant, we employed Price Waterhouse Business Turnaround Services. At Kayser-Roth and Topco, we hired Luther & Company.

Rule 10. Develop the short list of critical priorities and stick to it. At Cordiant, it was two things: stabilize clients and staff, and refinance the company. Accomplishing these two goals set the stage for everything else.

BOB'S WISDOM: Turnarounds are intensely difficult 24/7 situations. Follow the ten rules and you will prosper.

Quick! You've Got 100 Days to Act

When you move into any new role, but particularly in a turnaround situation, how you approach your first 100 days is critical.

During this time, you have "special permission" as the new guy on the block. After this period, you are seen as an ongoing participant in the organization and could indeed become part of the problem as opposed to leading the group's search for solutions.

It is important to use the first 100 days to set new standards and establish the right tone for the ongoing environment you want to do business in.

I try to establish high standards that commit the organization to growth, combined with an underlying tone of optimism, and the expectation that we will outcompete direct competitors.

Regarding the environment in which we will do business, I insist that we start with an open, honest, and candid assessment of the facts and use this as the basis for future success. I emphasize transparent and ongoing communications with clearly assigned roles, responsibilities, and accountabilities.

If there is a need for reconfiguring the organization with attendant redundancies, it is better to deal with these and put them behind you during the first 100 days. In general, you want to get the bad news behind you as quickly and thoroughly as possible, then start to build the future with your new team right away.

When I was bidding to acquire the Tetley worldwide tea and coffee assets from Allied Domecq, I had a list of eight things we were going to do in the first week that we owned the company. One of them was to shut down the U.S. headquarters and restructure the organization into two parts: a worldwide tea company managed from London, and a U.S. coffee company managed from the plant in Palisades Park, New Jersey. This would have been a key strategy with significant cost ramifications.

Our strategy had a high sense of urgency and was pegged to a three-year time frame. As it turned out, we finished second in the bidding and none of this ever happened. The winning bidder chose not to pursue our course and ended up selling the business after five years.

BOB'S WISDOM: Take advantage of the "special permission" inherent in your first 100 days and use it to set the right tone, direction, and cost base for the future.

Establishing Objectives, Strategies, and Plans

As a chief executive, it is your job to set a direction for the enterprise. Working with your team, you need to establish a clear vision or better yet, an inspirational dream that is specific to your situation and communicate it to everyone in the organization as often and as thoroughly as possible.

This also sets the stage for mapping objectives, strategies, and plans that bring your directions to life and focus the efforts of your people. The first questions to clarify are: What is an objective? What is a strategy? What is a plan? Organizations can become tied in knots if they do not get this simple structure right.

An objective can be described as a goal, an outcome, or an "end." It must be measurable. A strategy describes the boundaries you operate within to achieve the objectives. As such, they represent the "means to an end." A plan then is a set of action-oriented steps, taken in conformance with the strategies to achieve the objective.

If the objective is to "build share of market," the supporting strategy might be, "utilize promotional incentives to generate trial among non-users." A plan flowing from this could be, "circulate a direct mail coupon of 'x' value on 'y' date."

Setting strategies is particularly important. By establishing boundaries, strategies help channel the organization's efforts in the right direction and minimize unfettered thinking and actions. They provide the mechanism for evaluating the strength or sensibility of plans as they come forth. The simple question to ask is, "Is the plan on strategy?"

I harp on these definitions because improperly defining the objective, strategy, and plan invariably leads to sloppy thinking, poor execution, and negative results.

Consider the actions of politicians. Whether it involves their handling of the war in Iraq, or their response to Hurricane Katrina in New Orleans, politicians consistently make one or both of two errors. What they often refer to as strategies are actually objectives. When this happens, it leaves the listener wondering as to the means by which things will be accomplished.

Or, what they refer to as objectives are actually strategies. In response to Hurricane Katrina, "rebuilding the levees" would not be a properly framed objective. It is at best a strategy. A more relevant objective would be, "To keep water from flooding the city of New Orleans." Rebuilding the levees would be one of many strategies to consider as a means for achieving the desired outcome.

In a consumer goods enterprise, an annual budget is accompanied by an annual plan that details objectives, strategies, and action plans by division and by brand. Collectively, these represent the short-term steps on the path toward fulfilling the company's long-term vision or Inspirational Dream.

BOB'S WISDOM: If you do not know where you are going, any road will take you there. When steering your organization forward, focus clearly on objectives, strategies, and plans that get you to where you want to be.

Tape the Strategy to Your Forehead

When I was at Kayser-Roth, we received help with our turn-around strategy from John Luther of Luther & Company. John believed that strategies were not worth much unless they could be concisely distilled, easily understood, and refined to the point where people could "tape them to their forehead."

We worked hard to write a statement in twenty words or less that captured everything we wanted the company to be. Once we had it, we put it on tent cards, posters, t-shirts, and just about anything that we could place all around the company. Here is what the tent card said:

THE NEW KAYSER-ROTH VISION
Become the Best Leg Wear Company
By Meeting Customer and Consumer Requirements
Better and Faster than Competition
Through Total Quality

We used this statement to start off every meeting. Sometimes we collectively "took the pledge" by repeating the statement indicating we would do everything we possibly could in our individual jobs to help Kayser-Roth fulfill it.

The statement told everyone in the company much more than the twenty words alone. It told them that we were focused on being a leg wear company; we were resolved to be the best at what we had chosen to do; and the pathway to success would be meeting customer and consumer requirements. It committed us to meeting the stringent and specific demands of a Wal-Mart, as well as the more general demands of food/drug/mass retailers and department stores.

Regarding consumers, it meant understanding the high-fashion demands of the Calvin Klein woman and the everyday needs of the No Nonsense woman. It said we would benchmark everything we did versus competitors, that we were committed to offering superior products, and that we valued speed to market.

Finally, it committed us to using the Total Quality Process that we had invested in as the framework for everything we did.

In a world where you can debate strategy ad infinitum, the one thing that was not debatable was whether every person in the company knew what we wanted to accomplish. We reached the point where they could tape it to their foreheads.

BOB'S WISDOM: Get your strategic vision for the company down to twenty words or less and communicate it to everyone in the company as simply and as often as you can.

Perfecting 100 Day Plans

Most companies have strategic plans and annual plans. At Saatchi & Saatchi, we have strategic objectives and annual plans, but the one thing we use consistently is what we call a "100 Day Plan."

We started this back in 1997 when we demerged from Cordiant and relaunched ourselves as Saatchi & Saatchi PLC on the London and New York Stock Exchanges. We knew that as a new listing we would be watched closely and that a premium would be attached to high performance.

In our view, the attainment of our long-term goals for the company was predicated on our ability to execute a series of short-term strategic actions. We started with our first 100 Day Plan—the key things that we needed to accomplish in the next 100 days to be on track. There should be at least six and no more than ten objectives, and each one should start off with an action verb (e.g., "Win the XYZ account").

We shared our 100 Day Plan with our Board, which gave the plan high saliency in the organization. We also cascaded the plan across the entire enterprise.

We were like an American college football team with a twelve-game season. If you focus on winning every Saturday, before you know it, you have a 12–0 record for the season!

BOB'S WISDOM: A 100 Day Plan is a great technique for achieving long-term progress from a continuous series of short-term accomplishments.

What Does It Take to Get to the Top?

Red Auerbach won nine National Basketball Association titles, including eight straight from 1959 to 1966 as Head Coach of the Boston Celtics. When he met with our General Foods group, he let us in on the question he used to ask himself at the end of every season. Red felt too many teams asked the wrong question, "How can we improve next year's performance?" For some of them, this could mean moving up from eighth to seventh place. In contrast, the question Red always asked himself was, "What will it take to win the NBA Championship next season?"

This question did not focus on incremental change or minor improvement. Rather, it meant that Red was already preparing to do whatever was necessary for the Celtics to be crowned champions again the following year.

Too often, tinkering around the edges and not being prepared to do what is necessary to lead the field is a shortsighted perspective. The right question to ask is, "What does it take to get to the top?"

Publicis Groupe is a good example of the way a company should go about this. In 1999, they were essentially a France-based advertising network. Today, as a result of the vision and courage of Elisabeth Badinter and Maurice Lévy, Publicis Groupe—through strategic acquisitions—has built three worldwide advertising networks, the best media assets in its industry, and the leading healthcare and digital networks. Overall, it ranks fourth in the half trillion-dollar global marketing communications industry. All this resulted from asking the right questions.

BOB'S WISDOM: Do not waste time and resources on incremental change. Ask what it takes to get to the top and start climbing right away.

63

Don't Ask, "What's Wrong?"
Ask, "What's Right?"

When people come into an underperforming company, they often start by asking themselves, "What's wrong?" This is the opposite of what they should do. In my experience, the best starting point is to ask, "What's right?" Most enterprises that prosper do so for good reasons, and these reasons form the foundation from which you can and must build a successful company.

The Saatchi brothers left the company that bore their name following the investor revolt of 1994. I entered the scene as Chief Executive Officer Worldwide at the holding company level in July 1995. After stabilizing clients and staff and refinancing the company, we hired someone to fill the Saatchi & Saatchi network CEO job. This individual came to us with a good deal of industry experience, but unfortunately, he also came in thinking he knew all the answers and had little regard for the history of Saatchi & Saatchi. He exited within six months.

When Kevin Roberts joined us in May 1997, he had been a client of the agency for 20 years and was acutely aware of its strengths. He came in with a strategy of linking past, present, and future.

The Saatchi brothers had built a formidable agency based on three pillars. The first was the mantra of the company—"Nothing Is Impossible." The second was a hiring policy that only brought on people who were passionate, competitive, and restless. The third pillar was the understanding that the company was all about the work—the creative product—and the extent to which it met the client's business goals. Kevin embraced and maintained these attributes, and they became the links to the past.

To address the issues we faced in the present, we added two enhancements. The first was the rather audacious idea that we would no longer be just an advertising agency. Rather, we would reposition ourselves as an "Ideas Company." Ideas, of course, are the underlying strength of what become great ads and the fuel for transforming a client's business. Second, as a worldwide network, we built in the notion of "One Team, One Dream." We would all be together in the same boat, acting in our clients' interests.

Now we are moving toward the future, and this future is built on the concept of Lovemarks—the future beyond brands. We seek to create loyalty beyond reason for our clients' brands, businesses, and reputations by building on emotional connections rooted in mystery, sensuality, and intimacy. This future is being built on the pillars of the past and the enhancements of the last decade.

BOB'S WISDOM: Taking the best of the past, and linking it to the present and desired future is the most dynamic way to build a business.

Sometimes You Have to Blow Up the Old and Start Anew

I arrived at the original Saatchi & Saatchi PLC after the founding brothers were gone, and it had been renamed Cordiant. It consisted of the Saatchi & Saatchi and Bates worldwide advertising networks, Zenith Media, and a half-dozen other marketing services companies.

On day one, I visited the London headquarters of all the major units to introduce myself. I let them know who I was, my background, why I was there, and my thoughts about the company; and I told them how we were going to proceed initially.

I then asked the individual company heads to gather together everyone they considered to be relevant for me to meet with. At Saatchi & Saatchi, this was about 100 people in a huge conference room. They were young, old, tall, short, thin, stocky, men, and women. Overall, it was a pretty diverse group. I can still picture the guy standing directly in front of me. He was wearing a tie-dyed T-shirt and had green hair.

Following that, I went over to Bates. They had gathered about a dozen people in the boardroom—all men, older rather than younger, and all dressed in business suits. I thought to myself, "Wow! And these two companies are in the same business?"

Over the course of several months, I discovered that, basically, we had a dysfunctional company. The employees were bruised and battered by the turmoil of the past and its associated financial restructuring. Stock options had been underwater for years. The companies in the group were as opposite as oil and water. Everyone liked their individual enterprise, but saw no value in the broader holding company. In truth, they did not really want to be a part of it.

We had to carefully strategize for the future. Rather than try to make a silk purse out of a sow's ear, we chose to "blow up the old, and start anew." We recognized that the individual organizations within the holding group each had distinct cultures and values, but the combination added up to less than the sum of the parts.

Technically, we demerged the company. Saatchi & Saatchi and Bates went their separate ways, with each of them owning 50% of Zenith, the media company. The marketing services companies went along with one group or the other. For every two shares investors had in the Cordiant holding company, they received one in the new Saatchi & Saatchi PLC and one in Bates.

This gave everyone a new lease on life and a chance to start afresh. The new companies could link past, present, and future by using the positive aspects of their past as a launching pad. Everyone was free to concentrate on the excitement of the future rather than dwelling on the rancor and turmoil of the recent years.

For Saatchi & Saatchi, demerging allowed us to focus on our Inspirational Dream "to be revered as the hothouse for world-changing creative ideas". Three years later, we concluded a merger with Publicis Groupe of France at a share price that was 450% higher than our starting level. We have had financial improvement every year since then, and in 2008 Saatchi & Saatchi had the best year in the history of the company.

BOB'S WISDOM: Once you've identified the company's best resources, blowing up the old and beginning anew can be the fastest way to put a troublesome past behind you.

"Don't Get Fat-Headed by Winning"

As the coach of the Ohio State football team, Woody Hayes won 13 Big Ten titles, coached 56 All-Americans, had three Heisman Trophy winners, and amassed an overall record of 238–72–10. He told our General Foods group that he was most proud of the fact that over the course of his coaching career, he lost two games in a row only three times.

To Woody, the important thing was, "Don't get fat-headed by winning, because it is consistency of winning that counts."

This is great counsel in today's incredibly competitive world. All too often, a company is on top one day, and then falls by the wayside the next. Yes, you want your organization to have a great year, but as soon as one year is over, the next one is beginning, so there is no time to rest on your laurels.

This is also important when formulating objectives. At Saatchi & Saatchi, we compete aggressively for advertising awards, with the highlight of every year being our performance at the Cannes International Advertising Festival. Sure, we would like to be the overall winner every time, but our ongoing objective is to always be in contention and finish in the top three, as we have done most years in the past decade. For us, it is consistency in winning that counts. For our clients, that translates into consistency of performance on the job.

BOB'S WISDOM: Winning consistently beats any single victory.

Choose Your Partners with Care

Shortly after joining Cordiant as Chief Executive Officer, I conducted an assessment of the worldwide advertising industry by dividing the agencies into three groups—worldwide, local, and a group I called, "unfortunately, caught in the middle." At that time, there were at least nineteen agencies that proudly declared themselves "worldwide networks." On closer examination, a number of them did not really have the necessary resources to warrant that mantle.

I asked myself, "How many worldwide networks does the world need?" Given the breadth of the industry and client conflict policies, I concluded that there was a bona fide need for at least eleven, which is still a lot, but it's not nineteen. Clearly, we could expect that in the not-too-distant future there would be consolidation in our industry.

In this context, and given the situation at Cordiant, our first order of business was to stabilize and refinance the company. Then, we de-merged the enterprise into its major component parts.

Saatchi & Saatchi flourished in this new configuration, but it wasn't long before the drumbeats of consolidation from my initial analysis were indeed coming true. We seized the initiative and determined that our partner of choice would be the Publicis Groupe.

The key reason was that we were strategically more important to them than we were to any other holding company. We would immediately transform them into a multi-network enterprise and put them on the world stage with strong advertising and media assets. In September 2000, we became part of the Publicis Groupe family of companies and never looked back.

We concluded early on that we did not want to be the last person at the consolidation dance without a partner. Better to select your partner of choice, and not be left alone or with an unsuitable partner when the music stops.

For us, at Saatchi & Saatchi, this all worked out extremely well. For others, the dance music of consolidation continued to play, but there were no good alternatives for the ride home.

BOB'S WISDOM: Don't be the last person at the dance without a partner when your industry is consolidating.

The Acquirer Has Rights

I have been part of two significant multinational corporate mergers. The first was the hostile takeover of General Foods by Philip Morris. The second was the friendly acquisition of Saatchi & Saatchi PLC by Publicis Groupe. The first experience prepared me for the second.

When Philip Morris took over General Foods, their management was sensitive to the fact that it was a hostile takeover, and they went overboard to be gracious. At the same time, there was a cadre of people within General Foods who wanted to pretend that life would go on as though nothing had happened, and to the greatest extent possible, it would be business as usual.

The situation was problematic and prompted initiatives to examine how the two individual companies operated with a view toward capturing the best of both. This largely proved to be an exercise in futility, wasted a lot of time, and in virtually all cases resulted in doing things the way Philip Morris wanted them done.

Naturally, this experience greatly affected my philosophy when we merged Saatchi & Saatchi into Publicis Groupe. I determined that we would maintain our distinctive culture and values as an independent network; but from an administrative standpoint, I made it clear that "the acquirer has rights" and from day one we would fold our activities into the way Publicis Groupe did business. We would go with their accounting methodology and their management processes and systems; and we would use all their resources, including their accountants, lawyers, investment bankers, and public relations people.

This was painful in certain areas where we thought we did things better than they did, but no matter—the larger prize was integrating into a new world of business and making it work as seamlessly and harmoniously as possible. We had a meeting of hearts and minds, so there was no time wasted and no second-guessing. Over time, in the areas where we had better ideas to contribute, we have exerted positive influences for change.

For six years, I served on the Publicis Groupe Conseil de Surveillance (the French Board), and Kevin Roberts has served continuously on the Directoire (the French Operating Committee).

Today, Saatchi & Saatchi is a high-performing network within the Publicis Groupe family of companies. We have been very happy with our choice of an acquirer and have exceeded the expectations that accompanied their investment in Saatchi & Saatchi. Not every transaction is so fortunate.

BOB'S WISDOM: When your company is acquired, adapt quickly and totally to the acquirer's way of doing business and go on from there.

Selecting the Right Formula
for a Joint Venture

Properly constructed, joint ventures can be vehicles for complementing your core capabilities, enabling your business to expand into new markets at a faster pace with lower investment, higher odds of success, and few of the natural complexities associated with an acquisition.

But, if poorly constructed, joint ventures can ensnare you in an enterprise that is frustrating, time consuming, and difficult to untangle.

The first critical element is having the right partner. Both sides must share the same vision and commitment to success, as well as having complementary assets that ensure significant synergies are possible. The stakes should be equally high for both sides.

Second, to create a great performance in a duet, one of the dancers must lead. This gets down to how you divide up and run the partnership. In my view, if the venture is strategically critical to your organization, then you should "take the point." That is, make it at least 51:49, or up. If the venture is not strategically critical, then you can "give the point," that is, accept 49:51, or down. No matter how it comes out, the key thing is to make sure that somebody is in charge.

What about 50:50? Can that formula work?

I have seen some joint ventures where 50:50 spelled disaster over time. Even if common goals were shared up front, as time went on, it seemed that no one could agree on anything and there was no clear mechanism for reaching a consensus that led to a resolution.

These negative situations were in large company settings where leadership roles and people inevitably change over time. In that circumstance, it is better to be decisive and take the point or give the point, up front.

In a smaller company setting, where the principals are involved and can be expected to be around for the long haul, 50:50 may be the only way to go. That way, both sides see themselves as equal partners. It is essential, however, that both sides share the same vision and have a clear understanding and agreement on relative roles and responsibilities.

BOB'S WISDOM: Joint ventures do work, but only if you pick the right partner and construct the right formula for ownership and making decisions.

Centralization and Decentralization Do Not Mix

Philip Morris acquired General Foods Corporation in 1985. It was a hostile acquisition because as a consumer goods company, General Foods did not want to become part of a tobacco enterprise. However, Philip Morris was awash in cash and needed to perpetuate the firm, so they went ahead with a tender offer at $120 a share. Within a few days, the majority of the stock moved into the hands of arbitrageurs, and soon it was all over. General Foods was no longer an independent company. Rather, it became a wholly-owned component of the Philip Morris Companies.

There were great differences between the two organizations.

General Foods was a wide-ranging food company with many diverse businesses. Some were billion-dollar international brands like Maxwell House Coffee, and some were local, highly seasonal $20 million-dollar brands like Certo and Sure-Jell pectin used to make jams and jellies.

General Foods spent significant time and other resources on recruitment and career development, and had extensive relationships with the best business schools in the country. Strategic planning was important, and countless hours were spent on strategy development with a comprehensive review process. The company had tremendous staff resources and a center of expertise on virtually any business topic known to the consumer goods business world. Overall, it had a distinct culture all its own.

Philip Morris, by contrast, was monolithic. They knew the tobacco business like the back of their hands, and no detail about it was too small to escape them. The company's great success came from riding the Marlboro Man around the world. With the exception of its acquisition of Miller Beer, tobacco was the only business of Philip Morris at that time.

Management teams from both organizations had innumerable meetings back and forth, but despite the best of intentions on both sides, this acquisition never turned out to be a happy marriage. There are probably many reasons why this was the case—different cultures, different people, different attitudes, different businesses, and on and on. My own explanation is quite simple—centralization and decentralization do not mix. You have to be one or the other.

General Foods, on the one hand, was a highly decentralized company. Operating decisions were made by country, by division, and by brand. The people at the top of the company had little or no involvement in day-to-day activities. The company was simply too diverse, so all the management processes were set up on the principle of decentralization.

On the other hand, Philip Morris was a highly centralized company. It was essentially in one business, and its Marlboro Man was a highly distinctive symbol worldwide. Centralized processes were set up to control execution details and ensure that no one messed up the formula.

Philip Morris had a New Products Development Committee. Its members were the Chairman and CEO, his two predecessors, the heads of U.S. and international operations, and the head of strategic planning. Its charter was to review all proposed packaging changes and new product alternatives before they entered the marketplace anywhere in the world.

Since this committee had historically been highly effective, they decided that its charter should be extended to cover General Foods products as well, with the committee enlarged to include the appropriate General Foods management personnel. At the first meeting, the General Foods materials illustrating all proposed packaging changes and new product entries worldwide had to be wheeled into the room on luggage carts. The meeting sank under its own weight. It simply made no sense for this level of management to be reviewing the latest promotional packaging for a variety of small brands.

Subsequently, Philip Morris also acquired Kraft Foods, one of the few highly centralized international food companies. It is most likely that the happiest day of the Philip Morris food companies' acquisition experience was the day that all the General Foods businesses were folded into the Kraft organization. They had finally found some like-minded centralized managers to watch over these disparate businesses, and decentralization was dead.

BOB'S WISDOM: Centralization and decentralization are the nitro and glycerin of management. Separately, either can work well. Mixing them is a recipe for disaster.

What's Your Inspirational Dream?

Lots of companies have a vision or mission statement. At Saatchi & Saatchi, we have an Inspirational Dream because dreams are more powerful than visions or missions. Kevin Roberts has said, "Martin Luther King, Jr. did not stand at the Lincoln Memorial and say, 'I have a Mission Statement.'"

Our Inspirational Dream captures the essence of who we are and what we are all about. Our Worldwide Creative Board, led by Bob Isherwood, wrote the original version in 1997. This is what it said:

Saatchi & Saatchi Inspirational Dream

"To be revered as the hothouse for world-changing creative ideas that transform the brands, businesses, and reputations of our clients."

This Inspirational Dream was so powerful it put Kevin Roberts over the top in his decision to join us. He was staying at the Beverly Hills Hotel in Los Angeles, and thinking about joining another company. I faxed him the document, along with the challenge— "Your Destiny Awaits You." He called back and said, "Who wouldn't want to join a company that does that?"

The Inspirational Dream should be kept as short as possible. It has to inspire, differentiate, and make sense to a variety of audiences. For Saatchi & Saatchi, the relevant groups are our employees, clients, and investors.

Our dream statement packs a lot into twenty words. First, it says we do not want to just do our work. Rather, we want to do it so well that we will be revered, or at least recognized, for what we do. This is not because we have big egos (albeit some might say we have plenty of those), but rather because we want to attract talented professionals and innovative clients to our enterprise.

Second, we want to be the hothouse for our kind of work—the place that gives birth to new ideas and new approaches, and is on the cutting edge of what is happening in the world.

Third, it says we want to generate big ideas—indeed, world-changing ideas—not just good ones.

Finally, it says we are a service organization to our clients, and our success is seen through the success of their brands, businesses, and reputations.

Our Inspirational Dream is a powerful statement. It is who we are. It is why people and clients come to us. It shapes everything we do.

BOB'S WISDOM: When crafting your Inspirational Dream, make sure it captures the essence of who you are and what you are about as an organization, then live it every day.

Heaven and Hell in Europe

In Europe, there is a story that makes the rounds about Heaven and Hell. It goes like this:

In Heaven, the French are the cooks, the English are the policemen, the Swiss are the bankers, the Germans are the mechanics, and the Italians are the lovers. In Hell, the French are the mechanics, the English are the cooks, the Swiss are the lovers, the Germans are the policemen, and the Italians are the bankers.

While there are obvious dangers in stereotyping, if there were not some truth in this story, it would not generate the inevitable head nods whenever it is told.

The point is despite the emergence of the European Union and its currency, the Euro, anyone who assumes that the EU is the "United States of Europe" is greatly mistaken.

And companies that build regional strategies without specific attention to the cultures, mores, and values of each country in the region commit great follies.

If you are in a consumer goods business, you would do well to recognize that your regional strategies should be planned and executed country by country, culture by culture.

By way of illustration, take that cup of coffee served to you in Italy and compare it with what you might receive in France. The preparation technology and taste outcomes that meet consumer's needs are completely different. Or, have you ever noticed that the name of the leading brand of ground coffee varies in virtually every major European country, and that the competitive framework changes as well? There's a country-by-country reason behind all these and the many other factors that create the differences marketers must be aware of and be prepared to accommodate. They may not be all the way to Heaven or Hell *per se* but the differences, seemingly, are that great!

BOB'S WISDOM: Do not build regional strategies based on assumptions of sameness. Understanding how consumers and markets differ from country to country is an imperative.

SECTION FOUR

Business Operations:
Looking beyond the Obvious

Luck Is What Happens
When Preparation Meets Opportunity

Woody Hayes told my staff at General Foods about a football game Ohio State won in the final seconds by recovering a fumble and going in for a touchdown.

After the game, he was approached by a sportswriter who commented, "Boy, you were really lucky to win, given that fumble at the end of the game." Woody shot back, "Luck, my foot. We practice recovering fumbles all the time. Luck is what happens when preparation meets opportunity."

I am sure that line did not originate with Woody, but he certainly is the one who passed it on to me, and it is a great piece of advice.

We had a story similar to Woody's when General Foods was the first to commercialize NutraSweet and used it to introduce Sugar-Free Kool-Aid, Crystal Light drink mix, and Sugar-Free Jell-O. Some people said we were lucky that NutraSweet was invented and approved. What they failed to realize was that we worked with the manufacturer for eight years developing formulations and the protocols for FDA approval. There was much more to our success with NutraSweet than luck.

You cannot control chance, but you can control your ability to manage a situation to best advantage when opportunity (or perhaps disaster) comes your way. For example, you can do role-playing or act out "what if" scenarios.

In the coffee business, we held an annual rehearsal regarding what we would do if a frost in Brazil disrupted the availability of our raw materials. We also successfully managed a product-tampering situation with Stove Top stuffing mix because we had previously opened lines of communication with resources that proved to be invaluable to us when the crisis occurred.

On the personal side, you can prepare yourself for advancement and broader responsibilities by consistently building competency in critical skills areas. With proper preparation, you can make yourself an attractive candidate so that if and when opportunity knocks, you'll be the one who stands out and is selected rather than the one who is passed over.

BOB'S WISDOM: You can make your own good luck by continuously preparing yourself to take advantage of opportunity when it knocks on the door.

The Scarcest Resource of All

The emergence of the personal computer, the internet, and mobile communications has revolutionized how many people conduct business day-to-day, while also affecting the overall level of individual productivity and the manner in which we communicate with each other.

However, the explosion in use of e-mail, cell phones, and personal digital assistants such as the BlackBerry has a potentially significant downside—encouraging people to spend most of their time on what turns out to be the urgent rather than the important issues of the day. All too often, people react to these various communication devices instead of remaining in control of how they spend their time.

Time is the scarcest resource of all, yet it is the only one we each have in equal amounts. We have the same 24 hours in a day, seven days in a week, and 365 days in a year. How well you use your time will be a key determinant of your success.

To manage your time properly in today's environment, the first thing you should do is perfect the discipline of writing 100 Day Plans. This will give you a continual update of the key six-to-ten goals you need to accomplish in the upcoming three months. Simply put, if an activity does not relate to accomplishing your 100 Day Plan, do not allocate it any time. Target a minimum of two-thirds of your time toward achieving the objectives in your 100 Day Plan.

I handle e-mail by setting aside specific time periods to read and deal with it. Thus I avoid falling into the trap of continuously checking my inbox and diverting my time and attention.

As for your mobile telephone, try turning it off and dealing with messages instead of being continually disturbed and engulfed in extraneous conversations.

In an information overload environment, you need to exercise significant discipline to manage your time strategically and effectively.

BOB'S WISDOM: Everyone has the same amount of time, but people who decisively separate the important from the urgent matters of the day end up with more of it.

Generating Great Ideas

G rowth is a business imperative, and the lifeblood of a growing business is great ideas.

To create a flow, you have to set expectations that people will come forth with great contributions that are recognized and rewarded accordingly. You also need to accept that periodic failure is a valued by-product of an organization that generates great ideas as a core function.

You also need to recognize that ideas can come from anywhere and encourage behaviors that bring them forth.

At Saatchi & Saatchi, we positioned ourselves as an "Ideas Company." Accordingly, it is the job of everyone in our employ to be part of the ideas generation process.

When we launched Delta Air Lines' new Business Class Service in 1997, we did so with a "living billboard" in the middle of Times Square in New York City. Passersby could actually walk up and sit in the new seats in full view of the teeming crowd. This idea came from the Media Department—not the Creative Department—even though it was a devilishly insightful creative idea.

At Saatchi & Saatchi in Geneva, Switzerland, they have a "Fifteens" program whereby all employees spend 15 minutes of every day on a subject of their choice. This program generates great ideas that we use for our clients. It is just one example of how a formalized program can be established to encourage idea generation.

Procter & Gamble also have a good example of how great ideas can come from anywhere. In 2000, it became clear to them that an "invent it yourself" model was no longer capable of sustaining high levels of top-line innovation and growth. Accordingly, they created a "connect and develop" innovation model that leverages the capabilities of their own

7,500 researchers by linking with and tapping into the creative thinking of as many as 1.5 million outside inventors. By 2006, 35% of their new products in market had elements that originated outside P&G. Research and development productivity dramatically improved, and their innovation success rate more than doubled.

BOB'S WISDOM: Great ideas can come from anywhere, so expect and encourage them from everyone.

Cultivating Big Ideas

G reat ideas rarely come to you in their final form on day one. Rather, they start as seeds that are planted, watered, fertilized, pruned, and cultivated to produce something beautiful—just like flowers.

As an example, let's take one of the biggest marketing ideas of our time—Lovemarks.

Kevin Roberts is the impetus behind this idea. Kevin is a real thought leader in our industry and in this case, he became concerned that brands were running out of juice. The proliferation of brands and the sophistication of marketers had wrung most of the advantages out of traditional brand management. So Kevin asked himself a big question, "What comes after brands?"

He saw brands as commanding respect, but he saw a greater force in the power of emotion. Mystery, sensuality, and intimacy could help power loyalty beyond reason, but the greatest emotion of all was love. If only brands could get beyond respect and on the road to love, all could be well. Kevin continuously talked with others about this notion; he explored it in articles and speeches—initially thinking of it as "Trustmarks"—and kept probing the subject in his mind.

One evening, Kevin and I were waiting at Auckland International Airport in New Zealand on our way to Los Angeles, and he started on his Love rap. I had heard much of it before, but this time he pulled out a napkin and drew a horizontal line showing Respect at one end and Love at the other. He told me how brands needed to evolve from respect into something more—moving from one end of his line to the other—from respect to love.

I looked at it for a couple of minutes, and then drawing on my economics and business school training, offered, "There's another way to show this to more effect." I drew a second line, crossing over his Love/Respect line midway. His line was transformed in an instant into the Love/Respect Axis.

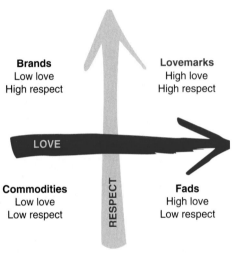

Kevin called this Lovemarks, and it is already a billion-dollar idea for the company. The Love/Respect Axis is the best conversation starter I have seen in business. Ask the question, "Would you prefer to be liked, or loved?" and there is universal engagement. Everyone immediately wants to know how they rate by measures of Love and Respect. We now have both methods and metrics supporting the Love/Respect Axis, and it has become an everyday tool in the Saatchi & Saatchi worldwide network.

BOB'S WISDOM: Cultivating big ideas is a lot like growing flowers. They have to be planted, fertilized, watered, and watched over with tender loving care before they blossom.

The Importance of
Excellence in Execution

Iconsistently try to establish a climate in which great ideas are expected to come forth. When they do, we properly resource them, and importantly, we recognize and reward our people who generate them.

However, I also ask that as people generate ideas, they should be prepared to stick around, spending the necessary time on the details and ensuring excellence in execution.

In my experience, a great idea poorly executed is worse than no idea at all because it consumes a lot of time, costs a lot of money, and usually fails.

All too often, a new product launch fails because the retail execution is not properly coordinated with the start of advertising. The advertising happens, people become aware of and interested in the product, but when they go to the store, it is not there; and by the time it does get there, consumers have already forgotten about it.

High-performing organizations pay attention to details and focus on excellence in execution. They recognize the tremendous leverage in this area. Paying attention to the smallest details and ensuring excellence in execution were a hallmark of the Philip Morris Companies, and one of the major reasons underlying the success of their core business.

Wal-Mart is similar as a retailer. They built their business on the idea "Always the low price," but it is the capabilities of their organization and the superiority of their systems that ensure the right product is in the right place at the right price at the right time. Again, no detail is left to chance.

BOB'S WISDOM: A great idea, poorly executed, is worse than no idea at all.

Cutting the Tail Off the Dog

A short-term focus can often place undue emphasis on cost-reduction activities including changes to a product formula, which is dangerous territory to navigate.

In year one, a brand may find that "lower cost Formula B" is perceived to be at parity to "original Formula A" and on that basis, a move is made to Formula B.

The next year, a new manager determines that "new, lower cost Formula C" is at parity to Formula B, and again a change is made. And on and on it goes, with each change being measured at parity to the preceding formula.

Over time, however, data that raises concern about the latest product's acceptance or preference begins to drift in. At this point, some down-the-line manager finds the gumption to test what by then is "new Formula E" in comparison to the "original Formula A" and finds, lo and behold, that they are not at parity at all.

Rather, the tail has been cut off the dog one inch at a time, as the expression goes, and original Formula A is dramatically preferred to the latest version in the marketplace!

Without malice or forethought, a series of cost-driven changes has unwittingly allowed a negative formula into the marketplace.

The way to prevent this is to ensure that any proposed formula change is always tested against three benchmarks:

1. The current marketplace formula
2. The Gold Standard (original Formula A)
3. The competition

Only those changes that maintain parity between the current formula and the Gold Standard, as well as preference versus the competition, should be allowed into the marketplace.

BOB'S WISDOM: Be wary of incrementalism. Don't cut the tail off the dog one inch at a time.

The Importance of Being First to Market

Early in my product management career at General Foods, I attended a presentation on new product introductions put on by A.C. Nielsen, the retail auditing company. It indicated that when a new market segment emerged, the first brand in—assuming it was at least a parity product—would get a 60% share of the resultant market. Subsequent entries would then divide up the other 40%.

This finding led me to always value speed to market, even when my organization did not have the original idea.

In 1972, I was the Product Group Manager for the Gaines line of soft-moist dog foods including brands like Gaines Burgers, Prime, Prime Variety, and Top Choice. Our primary competitor was Ken-L Ration from the Quaker Oats Company. They introduced a product called Ken-L Ration Cheeseburgers into test market. It was enjoying great success and they clearly had plans to expand, but appeared to have capacity constraints because their rollout plan was region by region, as opposed to a national introduction.

We decided to beat them to market in as much of the country as we could. We flew our marketing group to Kankakee, Illinois, to meet with our research and operations people, and together we quickly developed our own version of a cheeseburger product. As it turned out, we were first to market with Gaines Burger Cheeseburgers in 60% of the country, and Ken-L Ration Cheeseburgers was first in only 40%. True to the Nielsen findings, the first brand in ended up as the share leader.

In 1980, I was President of the Maxwell House Coffee Division when Folgers and other regional roasters introduced "high yield" coffees into test market. High yield meant that 13 ounces of the new coffee would brew as many cups in-home as 16 ounces of traditionally roasted coffee. While there was a risk that all these products would accomplish would be to lower the price of coffee, we determined that if they were going to be in the marketplace, then we had to be the first manufacturer to offer them. We developed our own high-yield roasting technology and commercialized it with the national introduction of Maxwell House Master Blend. We ended up being first to market and the year-one introduction exceeded $150 million in sales. Subsequently, virtually all supermarket coffee brands converted to high-yield varieties.

In today's marketing environment, the "window of exclusivity" for a new entrant is getting shorter and shorter. However, it remains true that the first brand in gets the lion's share of the business.

BOB'S WISDOM: Being first to market with the best product positions your brand to be the market leader.

"Three Yards and a Cloud of Dust"

Successful organizations do not stray from the fundamentals of their business.

Coach Woody Hayes' offense at Ohio State was often described as "three yards and a cloud of dust." It may not have been the most exciting action to watch, but it sure was an effective offensive strategy. To Woody, the fundamentals were blocking and tackling. He mostly stayed away from the pass because two bad things could happen—it could be incomplete or intercepted.

One of his messages to my staff at General Foods was, "Focus on fundamentals. Do not make mistakes and give the competition an unexpected advantage."

For a consumer goods company, the fundamentals start with the "Four P's"—Product, Positioning, Packaging, and Pricing. I know this is Marketing 101, but it is so fundamental, I believe it should be stated emphatically here.

Product is what you are selling to meet a consumer need. If your product is preferred to your competitors' in delivering what the consumer wants, you are one-quarter of the way to achieving the market leader position. The greatest difficulty with respect to product superiority is that worldwide, competitors work overtime to copy innovations as quickly as possible. Companies like Procter & Gamble devote untold time, attention, and resources to staying out in front and on the initiative with their product lines. It is a key underpinning of their success.

Positioning involves how you present your product to the consumer. It defines your target audience, your competitive frame of reference, your messaging, and your point of difference in meeting a consumer need.

It is the critical starting point for your communications program and for differentiating your product in the consumer's mind.

Packaging is the delivery device for presenting your product to the consumer, both in retail stores and online—what Procter & Gamble calls the "first moment of truth." In the current marketing environment, the package is more important than ever. Packaging needs to be cost-efficient to manufacture, functional for the retailer, informative to the consumer, sustainably produced and wonderfully designed. Too many packages fail on at least one of these fronts.

Pricing is what you charge the consumer. It needs to be properly aligned versus the competition, achieve appropriate profit margins relative to production costs, and represent good value to the consumer.

Putting these Four P's in place may seem elementary, but unless you get all four of them right every time, everything else you do, especially as a consumer goods company, will be inefficient and ineffective.

BOB'S WISDOM: Winning demands getting all the fundamentals right all the time.

One-Third of Consumers Do
Two-Thirds of the Consuming

As a rule of thumb in consumer packaged goods marketing, one-third of the buyers for any brand account for two-thirds of the consumption. These people are called the "heavy users." I have seen situations where it is even more concentrated, with as few as 20% of buyers accounting for 80% of consumption.

Sometimes we marvel at how much the heavy users actually consume. With Kool-Aid drink mix, it seemed at times that the heavy users might be taking baths in it as well as drinking it to quench their thirst.

At any rate, the heavy user groups are the people you want to research and understand to the last detail. You need to comprehend their mindset, their habits, and every aspect about how they use the product and the role it plays in their lives. Without their ongoing support, you can hardly expect to move your business in a positive direction.

Conversely, with a deep understanding of their behavior, you have the fuel for generating ideas that propel and maintain positive results.

Understanding the heavy users' reaction is particularly important when contemplating changes in a product's formula. Such changes must always be tested carefully among this group. I do not know how the Coca-Cola Company went about researching "New Coke" in 1985, but it is hard to understand why careful research among heavy users did not expose the debacle that ultimately ensued in the marketplace when it was launched.

The concept of heavy users and their importance have now penetrated our political system, with both Democratic and Republican candidates reaching out to their "base."

These are the people who are committed; they regularly make a lot of noise about individual issues, and rally together to get out the vote.

Without the support of the base, politicians find it difficult to win elections. Without heavy users, brands find it difficult to remain strong in the consumer-driven marketplace.

BOB'S WISDOM: Identify and understand every last detail about the frequent users for your product or service and use this knowledge to build your business.

Ninety-Five Percent of Winning Is Anticipation

Another bit of wisdom from Woody Hayes was, "Ninety-five percent of winning is anticipating what the other team will do." For Woody, this translated into a game plan whereby his offensive squad exploited the other team's weaknesses, and his defensive squad anticipated which plays the opposition was likely to run.

We translated Woody's message to mean that we needed to gain a better understanding of our business competitors, so we established a position titled "Manager of Competitive Analysis." When I first approached a candidate about taking this new role, he was unsure what the job entailed.

I said to him, "Let me illustrate by analogy. Let's pretend that we hired one of the notorious Watergate plumbers to break into the headquarters of our competition and steal their Annual Plan and their Strategic Plan. Amazingly, he brought us back documents that were identical to those you had created using only public sources of information." The candidate immediately said, "I've got it!"

Before we knew it, we had as good an understanding of our competitor's finances and operational capabilities as we did our own. We usually knew what they were going to do before they did it.

Woody would have been proud!

BOB'S WISDOM: Understand your competitors as well as you know yourself, and do not hesitate to exploit their weaknesses.

How to Defend Against a Competitor's Attack

Successful brands invite competition and everyone wants in on the action. When you face a challenge from a competitor, no matter how successful you have been, you have to mount a "Defense Plan." Failure to do so can have long-lasting consequences.

Just ask the Scott Paper Company, whose entire future was changed for the worse when Procter & Gamble entered the paper business.

I faced this challenge three times during my career at General Foods—with Cool Whip frozen topping, Stove Top stuffing and Maxwell House coffee. These were $100 million to $1 billion brands.

The competitive entrants were from Kraft, General Mills, and Procter & Gamble, respectively. Fortunately, each of the new entrants was at best a parity product. Accordingly, our defense plan consisted of four elements:

1. We chose to out-advertise the new entrant by a ratio of at least 1.5:1.

2. We attracted our users to be "out of the market" by preempting the new entrant's trial device with an effort of our own, and by linking this to repurchase incentives packed in our products.

3. We chose to match the new entrant's trade promotional offers, thus keeping the trade on our side.

4. We set up a war room with meetings every Friday during the six-month introductory period to ensure timely communications and excellence in execution on our part.

The net result was that in coffee, we held share in the face of the new competitor, and with the other two products, the new entrants never got off the ground. This all cost money in the short term, but in the long run, it was a great investment.

BOB'S WISDOM: Being safe is better than feeling sorry. Invest in a defense plan to ensure competitive survival.

"And/And" Beats "Either/Or"

Two of Kevin Roberts' favorite words in business are "and/and." We hear them all the time at Saatchi & Saatchi, and it keeps us from going down the wrong road of either/or.

And/and is a way of facing the continuing opposing choices that business managers have to make. It allows them to work with two complex opposites at the same time in such a way as to enhance each other. Or generate a new idea to consider.

So, if we are in a budget meeting, and someone says, "Either we can grow revenue or improve margins, but we cannot do both," we know this is the wrong answer. We must do both to be successful.

Or, if we are in a meeting about new media, and someone says that the internet will make television obsolete (just as people once thought television would make radio obsolete), again, we know this is the wrong answer. The reality is that both will coexist. Yes, new media has emerged, but television is not going away. In fact, it remains very strong and is influencing the content of the web just as the web is becoming a delivery system for television programs.

Our Toyota client is a master of and/and. They embrace the best practices of both the Japanese and American management styles, while refusing to compromise on either. They embrace the long and short term with a clear vision for 2020, while passionately focusing on daily sales. They embrace continuous innovation and cost reduction with new models that are often roomier, more powerful, lighter, more fuel efficient and have more features, while remaining cost-effective for the consumer.

The world usually is not black and white—it is gray (and blue and green and red and yellow and pink), so you would do well to deal with it on that basis.

BOB'S WISDOM: Avoid either/or. The correct answer most of the time is and/and.

Layoffs Are Hard

When I arrived in Greensboro, North Carolina to head up Kayser-Roth, I discovered they had two plants that supplied yarn to the sheer hosiery operations. The plants had been invested in years earlier on the premise that they would be vertically integrated cost-reduction facilities. Now, they were candidates for closure.

Investments based on vertical integration can go bad over time. They initially look attractive as they cut out a supplier and offer a lower cost product using known technology and equipment at a particular moment in time. Over time, however, you usually fail to maintain the investments and keep them at the cutting edge of the industry simply because they do not represent your core business. New technologies emerge, suppliers who are in that core business invest and innovate, and you end up with an asset trap. That was the situation I inherited. The question was, "What to do?"

The people at the plants involved were keenly aware of the situation. One day, I received a heartfelt, well-written letter from the spouse of a plant employee urging me not to shut down the facility. She talked about her husband's long service, his loyalty to the company, and her fear of what might happen to them if the plant closed.

The letter was powerful enough to cause me to take the time to reflect on what we were doing. Who was I to come in as the new guy and make such a decision that would, indeed, adversely affect many people's lives?

I concluded that realistically, I had a higher obligation and a larger role to play in the future of the company. Fundamentally, it was my job to make Kayser-Roth a great place for those employees continuing on. Shutting down the uneconomical plant would be an unfortunate situation for those affected, but it would be wasteful for the shareholders and unfair to all the other employees in the company to continue subsidizing an activity that was no longer profitable. Such is the dilemma of the Chief Executive Officer.

I responded to the woman who wrote the letter by thanking her for her input. We closed the two facilities, but were sensitive and careful about how we handled the situation. One of the plants was sold as a going concern to a supplier and the employees were protected in the purchase agreement. The other plant was shut down and the employees were treated as fairly as possible in terms of severance, retraining, and opportunities for transfers.

BOB'S WISDOM: Closing a plant is a sad day, so treat the people adversely affected as fairly as possible. Your larger obligation though, is to make the company a great place for the employees who are staying on.

What Separates a Great
Ad from a Good Ad

When I started my business career in product management at General Foods, my initial tasks focused on volume and Nielsen data analysis, sales activities, and promotion plans. As I moved up to become an Associate Product Manager, I began accompanying my boss to the agencies to learn the artful job of commenting on advertising.

The company also had specially designed training programs to assist in this process. One day, I was attending a copy seminar put on by one of our agencies.

We were chatting with the Creative Director, and I remarked, "You get presented a lot of ads. How do you tell a good one from a bad one?" He replied, "I always ask myself the same question. Does it make the right point clearly, and in an interesting way?" I thought to myself, if this approach works for him, maybe I should try it.

For the next 25 years as a client, when presented with an ad, I asked myself the Creative Director's question.

"Does it make the right point?" is another way of asking, "Is the ad on strategy?" Brands spend a lot of time sorting out strategic direction, and the first obligation of an ad is to be in conformance with the chosen direction. The second point, "clearly," simply reflects that most of us lead busy lives and if an ad is at all confusing or lacks clarity, it is unlikely to be successful. The third point, "in an interesting way," is usually where the action is. An ad has to break through the clutter, engage the viewer, and ultimately be believable, memorable, and persuasive. The elements that create "an interesting way" help to do this and make you want to see the ad again.

In 1995 when I hopped over the fence from the client side to the agency side, I met Bob Isherwood, the Worldwide Creative Director for Saatchi & Saatchi. Bob was a giant in his field. In May 2007, I had the honor of attending a Clio ceremony in Miami, Florida, where he was awarded a Lifetime Achievement Award in recognition of his work. This was the latest in a long and much-deserved list of international honors for him.

Bob, I learned, wasn't interested in just producing good ads. That was easy. What Bob wanted were great ads! So, I asked him to define what constitutes a great ad. Here is what he said:

> "A great ad grabs you by the emotions,
> and then gives them a twist!"

BOB'S WISDOM: As a client, develop a reliable framework for evaluating ads and then only go for the great ones.

Secrets to Client Success

For the first 28 years of my career, I was a consumer packaged goods advertising client. I spent more than $2 billion in measured media on more than 60 brands, working with seven different agencies. I have been active on the agency side at Saatchi & Saatchi in one capacity or another for 14 years.

All in all, I have watched agencies and clients interact from both sides of the fence for at least 40 years, so I ought to know something about the factors that lead to client satisfaction. At Saatchi & Saatchi, we try to create and keep what we call "PICs"—permanently infatuated clients.

My first observation regarding how to succeed at this stems from my days as a client. The agency must never lose sight of the reason they were hired in the first place. Clients hire agencies to access consumer insights, creative ideas, and superbly executed communications that build and grow their businesses.

This was brought to my attention in 1975, when Bill Phillips was the Chairman of Ogilvy & Mather at the same time that Maxim freeze-dried coffee was in my group at General Foods. Our advertising at the time was not achieving optimal impact. When we visited the agency, the account team began the meeting by presenting a promotion plan. This was not what we were expecting from our advertising agency. Bill came into the meeting, immediately sensed what was going on and said to his people, "Look, there is a poor living to be made in the ad agency business by presenting promotion plans to the client. Our first obligation is to develop great ads."

In today's integrated communications environment where many agencies offer a full portfolio of strategic communications services, this view is no longer the rule. But overall, it is still good advice to advertising agencies to put first things (great ads) first and always remember that the agency/client relationship is built on great ideas and creative communications that sell products.

I also emphasize here that the client appreciates an agency that is on the initiative and anticipates their needs, rather than one that sits back and only reacts to client requests.

At Saatchi & Saatchi, we know a lot about this because Procter & Gamble has been a client of the agency and its precursors for 88 years, General Mills for 85 years, and Toyota for 34 years. It is a challenge that requires constant attention to staffing, the quality of the work, and the agency's capabilities to meet the client's needs in ever-changing economic, social, and cultural environments.

People at the agency must know more about the brand and its equity than their client counterparts. Given today's rate of turnover in corporate personnel, the agency often represents continuity on the account and is also rightly expected to know more about consumer trends and changes in the communications environment than the client. The pace of change in today's world presents constant challenges and opportunities in that regard.

The agency needs to understand the management processes by which the client operates, and adapt its own work patterns to fit into those procedures. Fundamentally, the agency is serving the client—not the other way around.

The agency always benefits from a client's sound and comprehensive agency evaluation process. There is nothing like ongoing, open, honest, and candid feedback to help shape the relationship.

The agency must build relationships with the client from the top to the bottom of their organization. People change jobs, show up in other roles, and have different perspectives depending on their level in management. The agency needs to understand them all. There must also be someone at the highest level of the agency whom the client can go to at those moments when delicate matters require an immediate and decisive response.

These are the basic ingredients for a successful agency/client relationship. Once they are all in place, then, as a wise person at Saatchi & Saatchi once said:

> "Don't just give the client what they want, give them
> what they never dreamed possible!"

On a final note, there is a store in Westerly, Rhode Island, called Sandy's Fine Foods where Sarah and I shop when we are on vacation. They have a slogan printed on their grocery bags that sums up the secret to client success. It says, "We are family, and our customers always sit at the head of the table."

BOB'S WISDOM: Always put the client at the head of the table and deliver everything they hired you for in the first place.

"Who's Got the 'R'?"

When Kevin Roberts joined Saatchi & Saatchi in May 1997, he brought with him the RASCI management technique. It turned out to be the best process I have encountered for approaching decision making on complex subjects.

RASCI is an acronym for assigning roles and responsibilities on any given project. At Saatchi & Saatchi, we apply it as follows:

R = Responsible. The single person committed to drive the project or task. As a general principle, there is only one R.

A = Approve. The people (there can be more than one) who have the final sign-off on the project.

S = Support. These people help the R get the job done.

C = Consult. The R can call on these people for their advice. We add two rules: (1) a C has three days to respond to a question; (2) the R can ignore the advice.

I = Inform. The people who need to know about the project as it proceeds, but who are not C's.

For us, sometimes the R and the A are self-evident given the topic and the structure of our organization. But at other times, this is no simple matter. In our highly matrixed and geographically complex organization, it becomes more and more important to know how work will be done, both efficiently and effectively. Too often, people might either duplicate efforts that ultimately prove confusing, or worse, people could be standing around waiting for others to act. RASCI solves this problem for us with a clear, up-front designation of who will do what with whom.

Within Publicis Groupe, Procter & Gamble is the single largest worldwide client, and we have more than a dozen Global Equity Directors (GEDs) across three networks assigned to individual brands or categories. Often, a topic comes up that transcends all these GEDs, brands, and categories. By assigning a RASCI to the task, everyone understands clearly from day one which person is responsible for what.

At Saatchi & Saatchi, we have reached the point where RASCI is a way of life, and the first question anyone asks on a decision-making topic is, "Who's got the 'R'?"

BOB'S WISDOM: RASCI is a great management technique for clarifying roles and responsibilities in decision making.

SECTION FIVE

Finance and Economics, or Dollars and Sense

The Importance of Market Share Ratios

The best measure of strength for a consumer packaged goods brand is its volume share ratio versus its closest competitor. Your share of market represents the net effect of consumers voting at the store every day. To calculate your share ratio, simply divide the market share for your brand by the share of your closest competitor. Then compare it to the following chart that I developed, based on my own experiences:

RATIO	CATEGORY
3:1 and up	Undisputed leader with an economically leveraged position in market versus the competition
2:1	Sustainable franchise leader, but not one that enjoys significant economic leverage
1.5:1	Leader, but watch out, the next one can catch you with a strong initiative
1:1	Horse race

The place you want to be is in the first two categories. These are economically powerful and sustainable positions. The lower two categories require day-to-day monitoring of your position and the competition's every move.

If you fall on the wrong side of the preceding ratios, life is no fun. You will discover that with your competitors in the driver's seat, you are vulnerable to their every move.

BOB'S WISDOM: Your volume share ratio versus the next leading competitor is the key measure of your franchise strength. Get it to 2:1 or above and keep it there.

Breaking the Law of Diminishing Returns

If you study economics, you learn about the "Law of Diminishing Returns." *Barron's* defines it as "beyond a certain production level, productivity increases at a decreasing rate."

I have always thought of it more broadly and simply put: as time moves on, your propensity to grow or improve declines.

For example, I learned how to play golf at age 13. The first time I played I shot 109. By the end of my first year, I had shot an 85, or an improvement of 24 strokes. By the end of my second year, I had shot a 75, a further improvement, but of only 10 strokes. By the end of my third year, I had a 3 handicap although my improvement was in consistency, not in a significant further reduction in strokes. Today, I have a 9 handicap. I am going the other way!

Or, take a manufacturer who launches an initiative. In year one, he might improve his overall sales by more than 100%, but in year two, a further 50% improvement would be huge. As time goes on, the initiative requires careful management to grow at the market rate.

The Law of Diminishing Returns usually takes the shape of an "S" curve as shown on page 126.

The x on the graph marks the "point of inflection." Up to that point, growth or improvement is occurring at an increasing rate. After the x, it is at a declining rate.

What you must realize about the Law of Diminishing Returns is that it is universal in application to all situations. Think of a factor, any factor. Now think how this law applies to it. Initiatives may start out moving quickly, but inevitably they lose momentum.

Growth/Improvement versus Base

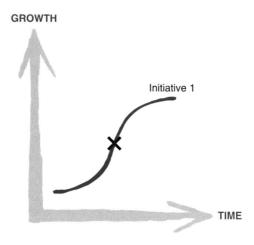

Historically, let's look at A&P and Sears, and for current examples, we can look at Wal-Mart and Microsoft. They are all great companies that have moved from quantum growth to incremental growth. Over the years, the Law of Diminishing Returns affects all companies. The impact is based on a question of time and degree. The more a company stands still or only modestly extends its current business, the sooner this fate will befall it.

So, the big question is, "If the Law of Diminishing Returns is universal in application, how do you keep growing and improving?" The answer is simple—you have to continuously hop onto a new curve! Just as your first curve is "topping off," you must be ready to launch a new initiative timed to get you onto a new curve. Graphically, it looks like this:

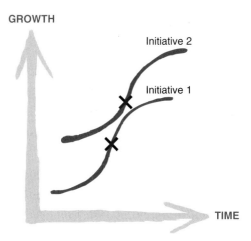

The key point is that as each initiative approaches the point where it is topping off, your next initiative is timed to pick up the slack and take you to a new level. This continuous process gives you the sum of the parts, with the most recent initiative providing the continuing growth impetus.

The best example of where this is happening today is with Apple. They introduced the iMac which was followed by iTunes, which was followed by the iPod, which was followed by the iPhone. Through a process of continuous innovation, they keep hopping onto a new curve from a strong foundation.

As the base of a company becomes incredibly large, it is correspondingly difficult for the new initiatives to be big enough to really move the total. The bigger the company, the greater the need for truly big ideas, and the tougher it is to beat the Law of Diminishing Returns.

BOB'S WISDOM: You can't stand still or the Law of Diminishing Returns will get you. Plan ahead and keep getting yourself onto a new curve.

How to Do Annual Planning

Annual planning in a consumer-packaged goods enterprise is a necessary and detailed process. It specifies the programs to be implemented, volume requirements by brand and size, budgets and headcount for all cost centers, marketing spend levels, and the overall profit expectation for the upcoming year.

For some companies, this can become an introspective process with a short-term outlook that overlooks a brand's connection to the marketplace. Such a negative scenario can innocently begin by management setting an overall annual profit growth goal for the company—say 10% versus a year ago—and before you know it, each and every brand is planning for a 10% profit increase.

The next negative step can occur when planners begin at the bottom of the profit and loss statement with a plus 10% profit expectation and work their way up. Under this approach, profit becomes the determinant of the action plan instead of the results of the organization's efforts. Before you know it, the focus is on short-term steps such as cost-reducing formulas, reduced marketing spends, and shifts from advertising to promotions accompanied by a corollary effect of reduced share or volume. The brand headed down this path is embarking on a course that I call "the vicious cycle of downside leverage."

The proper way to do annual planning is to insist that the process begin in the external world of consumers and competitors. Analyzing and meeting evolving consumer needs while anticipating what the competition will do is fundamental to success. Brand programs should be aimed at enhancing consumer preference and blunting competitive actions.

The quantification process should begin at the top of the profit and loss statement with customers and revenue based on a forecast of volume derived from market and share growth assumptions. Pricing, spending, and cost management activities should flow from agreed strategies, principles, and plans. The forecast of profit should be the result of everything you do, not the determinant.

When annual planning is done properly, it ensures your short-term profit goals as well as your long-term ambitions.

BOB'S WISDOM: Do the profit and loss statement from the top down, beginning in the external world of consumers and competition.

Don't Get Outfoxed by Low-Ballers

In March 1970, I began a one-year stint as the Washington, D.C., District Sales Manager for the Post Division of General Foods. It was designed to increase my exposure to customers and provide me with a new management dimension as well as a chance to see how headquarters worked (or did not) from the vantage point of a field location. It was a great experience.

There were 24 sales districts organized into five regions. I reported to a Regional Sales Manager who was responsible for five districts, each representing about 20% of the region's volume. At the end of the quarter, we had our usual meeting to confirm each District Manager's forecast of sales for the current quarter and review plans for the upcoming quarter.

Our collective forecasts were falling about 100,000 units short of the budget expectations. Determined to close the gap, the Regional Manager asked for volunteers to increase their sales estimate. Alternatively, he planned to assign new targets with the expectation that they would be delivered.

All of a sudden, the District Manager sitting next to me—a wily veteran known as "The Preacher"—leaped to his feet and launched into a monologue about how his men would rise to the challenge of delivering a higher number. Then he made it specific, "We will increase our estimate by 10,000 units!"

The next wily veteran promptly volunteered to match what The Preacher had offered.

I quickly did the math and saw what was happening. Instead of their fair share of the increase—20,000 units—the veterans were "volunteering" for half that amount. The rest of us had been snookered. We were now left with 80,000 units to be divided by three.

This rookie learned his lesson, and never again was I caught flat-footed or misled by low-ballers.

While this story occurred in a sales setting, you can find low-ballers in all organizations, particularly at budget-setting time, so you need to have a keen sense of what is doable and fair. When you are reaching for the last increment of performance, it is important that everyone fully contributes their fair share.

BOB'S WISDOM: When you set performance goals, ensure that everyone takes responsibility for their fair share.

Delivering Budgets in a
Client Organization

At General Foods, we always developed an annual budget—by brand, by category, by division, and by country. This set our volume, revenue, and earnings expectations for the year.

I used to think of these budgets and the assumptions they were based on as "our best thinking at a moment in time." What the company ultimately needed to achieve was the proper overall results in the context of the real-world market dynamics that occurred. Inevitably, the first day of the new fiscal year would come, and we would begin to measure variations versus the assumptions made in the budget and thereby start the process of making course corrections.

In no place was this truer than in the coffee business. The underlying component of our cost structure (the price of unroasted green coffee beans) had day-to-day commodity volatility that created cost and possibly pricing implications. Competitive spending might also vary—by element by brand, and by market. Additionally, there would often be some unanticipated event that required action.

Fortunately, we had a talented line organization and extensive staff resources to sort out these issues. Our managers included smart, highly analytical, left-brained individuals. I would charge them with exploring what I called "the infinite world of possible solutions." This meant they needed to be flexible and prepared to juggle all the variables versus original assumptions to ensure we came out with the desired overall results.

If the price of green coffee beans varied by type, we might run some alternative equivalent blends. If competitive spending ramped up on Brand A in Market 1, we might adjust spending up or down in Markets 2, 3, and 4. If an unanticipated event unfolded in the marketplace, we could respond by launching a new product variation of our own, or alter the timing on a previously planned initiative. We had to stay on top of real-world events and make sure we were flexible and responsive in dealing with them.

We wrote strategies based on long-term principles, but were constantly aware of how to vary execution to adapt to the realities of the market. In our planning, we ran many "what-if" scenarios to prepare us to deal with changes as they occurred.

This management process inevitably produced the desired end result.

BOB'S WISDOM: Managing the infinite world of possible solutions is the best way to deliver budgets in a client organization.

Achieving Budgets in an Advertising Agency

I knew that being on the agency side would be a very different experience from being on the client side, and that it would be especially so in setting budgets and managing the annual plan.

On the client side, we established budgets in a "bottom-up" manner, and management of the annual plan included staying on top of the infinite world of possible solutions. To achieve this, we had legions of highly analytical people and extensive financial support staff.

On the agency side, this is not the case at all. You are in a creative business that serves clients. Many financial variables are not under your control. Your assets are the people who go up and down the elevators every day, and your scarcest resource is the time it takes to generate a big idea and produce a great ad.

Therefore, it makes little sense to go through an extensive bottom-up budget process, and you certainly cannot rely on managing the "infinite world of possible solutions" to produce the desired end result as it pertains to earnings expectations.

Rather, you need to forecast a reasonable top-down projection of revenue, and set limits on the costs incurred in delivering that revenue projection. Inevitably, this extends to setting limits on headcount and deriving cost centers.

I call this "determining the pot of affordable resources." The juxtaposition of reasonable revenue projections and limits on the pot of affordable resources determines earnings in a service business.

You might ask, "How do you keep this from careening down into a never-ending spiral of fewer heads and cost reduction?" The answer is, you need to make sure that your organization is committed to and capable of growing revenue faster than the market rate, thereby growing market share.

This is because any well-run agency should be able to convert incremental revenue at a higher margin than is the case for the base business.

If the agency only grows revenues equal to the market it may offset inflation and keep abreast of competition, but it will accomplish little more than extending its current financial picture.

It is the ability to grow revenue faster than the market that produces the affordability to add people and accommodate higher costs while achieving higher margins and earnings.

BOB'S WISDOM: Growing revenues faster than the market rate and determining the pot of affordable resources are the keys to achieving budgets in an advertising organization.

"If I Knew What the Price of Green Coffee Was Going to Be Tomorrow, I Wouldn't Be Working Here"

When I was President of the Maxwell House Coffee Division at General Foods, one of my most valued staff members was our green coffee buyer, Paul Keating. Green coffee beans are the raw material that is roasted before being packaged as a finished product. Paul bought 600 million pounds of green coffee a year, making him the largest single coffee buyer in the world. He knew all the producers and commodity houses. Indeed, he knew more about green coffee than anyone on the planet.

One day we were talking about the forecast for green coffee prices and Paul said, "Look, if I knew what the price of green coffee was going to be tomorrow, I wouldn't be working here."

This simple but wise statement caused me to pause and reflect. If Paul knew more about the subject than anyone else, yet even he could not be sure, then indeed no one really knew! Just as with other commodity prices, foreign exchange, and stock prices, there is no such thing as certain knowledge. At best, there are informed judgments. Accordingly, all strategies must be capable of working both ways—how will we behave if the price goes up, and where will we be if it goes down?

The other question this left was, "How do we leverage our knowledge, if indeed, we know more about this than anyone else?"

We began by articulating possible buying strategies, and developed a benchmark model that pretended we bought 1/250 of our annual requirements every working day at whatever the price actually turned out to be. After analyzing our alternative strategies, we became convinced that we could outperform the model by about 7% or 4 cents a pound on an average price of 59 cents. In actuality, we outperformed the benchmark every year, and by measuring results versus a standard, we continuously improved our performance. Knowledge certainly proved to be worth something!

BOB'S WISDOM: With issues such as foreign exchange rates, commodities, and stock prices, you cannot really know what tomorrow will bring. Be prepared to deal with movement in either direction and leverage your unique knowledge.

There Are Three C's in Pricing

Setting the right price for your product or service, along with managing it properly over time, is one of the most important tasks in business. Price it too high and you may earn a high profit per unit but not sell very much product. Price it too low and you may sell a lot of units, but not make any money.

Every brand should have a disciplined pricing strategy. A good one will benchmark the price for your product to the "Three C's"—Competition, Costs, and the Consumer Value framework.

Let's use Jell-O brand gelatin as an example. The first benchmark would be a defined price differential per package to other branded and private label competitive products. Jell-O has a high market share and therefore can command a price premium, but it must be within defined boundaries.

The second benchmark would be relative to costs. The primary cost ingredients in Jell-O are sugar and gelatin, both of which have commodity price variations. However, these ingredients represent shared costs and the variations up and down must be covered by all manufacturers. The expectation for the cost-related benchmark would be that Jell-O would pass on cost variations and maintain profitability as a percentage of revenue.

The third benchmark would keep Jell-O in line with its overall value to the consumer. Jell-O is primarily a sweet food dessert alternative. Accordingly, we can create a composite price index for dessert alternatives and peg Jell-O to compete at a defined relationship to that index.

At times, the benchmark targets for the Three C's can run into conflict with each other. In such cases, priorities must be assigned. For most brands, maintaining the proper price relationship to the competition usually represents the highest priority.

A good pricing strategy also defines the pricing leader in the market. The best situation is for it to be your brand, leaving all the competitors to react to your strategy. Consistency of action is the key to this happening.

BOB'S WISDOM: A disciplined pricing strategy is essential to the financial health and competitive position of your product. Define benchmark targets for the Three C's and stick to them.

Adam Smith on Pricing

As an economics major at Harvard, I learned about Adam Smith's "law of supply and demand" whereby price is the factor that equates these two variables. A firsthand example at General Foods brought it to life for me.

I was an Associate Product Manager on TANG, the drink that went with the Apollo astronauts to the Moon. These were happy days for the brand. The bumper crop of Florida oranges was history and there were new opportunities for growth. I started my assignment three months before Wally Schirra took off on the first Apollo flight and ended it the Friday before Neil Armstrong stepped on the moon.

TANG was a replacement for frozen orange juice, and came packed in 7-, 18-, and 27-ounce glass jars. Consumers made it up primarily by the glass, mixing the appropriate amount of powder with the prescribed amount of water. The competition—frozen orange juice—came in 6-ounce cans that were mixed with water to make a 24-ounce batch.

All in all, two very different ways of getting a glass of orange taste and ingesting Vitamin C!

The wizards in our market research department had come up with a statistical model to predict TANG sales. They inputted advertising and promotion spending levels, and other information related to the market variables.

The model showed that despite all our impressive marketing activity, the primary correlation with sales still turned out to be what was called the "TANG/Frozen Orange Juice Price Differential" per reconstituted ounce. Just as in the laws of economics, the cheaper TANG was relative to frozen orange juice, the more we could expect to sell.

What was interesting about this finding was that given the differences in their physical nature and how the products were packaged and prepared, surely no consumers were actually doing the math to compare prices on a per reconstituted ounce basis. That calculation would have been virtually impossible. Rather, I concluded, consumers must have "infinite wisdom" regarding the price comparison. Perhaps it was an innate sense of how long TANG stayed in their cupboard versus frozen orange juice in the refrigerator.

Whatever the explanation, it was a real-life example that the laws of economics indeed are true, and that one must fully respect the wisdom of the consumer.

BOB'S WISDOM: The laws of economics are unassailable. Consumers have infinite wisdom on price.

SECTION SIX

Lessons in Leadership

What Is Leadership?

The topic of leadership is the subject of numerous books and studies. Despite all these efforts, it seems to retain a certain mystical or elusive quality.

I once looked in Webster's Dictionary for a definition. Under "leadership" it said, "the office or position of a leader." This was not very helpful, so I went to "leader." There it said, "A person who leads; a person who directs a military force or unit; and a person who has commanding authority or influence." I concluded that Webster did not know much about leadership.

The simplest definition I have heard is, "a leader is someone who has followers." I once used this definition when terminating an employee from a key leadership position. I said to him, "The simplest definition of a leader is someone who has followers, and the reality is that you do not have any." This stark statement spoke volumes about the nature of the problem and there was not a lot left to be said after that.

The most complete and articulate definition of leadership I have come across is by Mike Vance, a management consultant who speaks on the topic. He wrote:

> Leadership is the ability
> to establish standards
> and manage a creative
> climate where people are
> self-motivated toward
> the mastery of long-term
> constructive goals, in a

participatory environment
of mutual respect, compatible
with personal values.

The key words and phrases in this definition are: *establish standards, creative climate, self-motivated, mastery, long-term, participatory,* and *mutual respect.*

I took the job as President and CEO with Kayser-Roth because I believed the main ingredient the company was missing was the type of leadership that I could provide. In my first talk to the organization, I boldly stated, "I came here to play a leadership role in turning around the performance of this company." Then I focused on how to deliver on it.

A key task was to change everyone's concept of what constituted ideal performance. The company was mired down with a reputation as a low-performance, financially unhealthy enterprise. As Mike Vance would say, I had to "establish standards."

Before I could do this, I had to establish myself as a credible person worthy of the trust of the organization. As a leader, you cannot expect to have followers who support you without first establishing trust. My strategy for achieving this was to meet personally with every person in the company, and share with them my vision and expectations.

I set three initial expectations for all of us. The first was that our relationship would be characterized by openness, honesty, and mutual respect. The second was that people would accept a high degree of accountability for results in their areas and take the initiative in making things happen for the better. The third was to recognize that to be effective, I had to be well informed.

From the vantage point of these personal meetings, I began to learn intimate details about the company that helped me to determine the appropriate business direction, set objectives and strategies, and formulate plans for the future. These became the tangible vehicles for launching the concept of ideal performance and establishing standards.

Within two and one-half years we were a profitable, growing enterprise that ultimately became an attractive acquisition. Without the critical first step of laying the groundwork for exercising leadership and earning the trust of followers, it never would have happened.

BOB'S WISDOM: Leadership is intangible. The first step is earning the trust of people you work with. Everything else follows from that.

Chairmen and Chief Executives

I have worked for companies and served on the Board of Directors for enterprises in the United States, the United Kingdom, and France.

Naturally, each has its own distinctive business culture, and corporate governance varies considerably within and between the three countries. In the United States and France, companies tend to vest all power in the hands of a single Chairman and Chief Executive, whereas in the United Kingdom, they often separate the two functions.

The demands of running a public company in today's global business environment are greater than ever. Much of the recent literature on the subject suggests that the job has grown beyond the abilities of any one individual. There are, however, people who seem to handle the job on their own with aplomb.

Based on my own experience and the simple notion that two heads are better than one, I believe that dual roles are the way to go. This approach requires two strong, complementary individuals, each of whom has a clear understanding and acceptance of their relative roles and responsibilities, as well as an appreciation of respective personal strengths and weaknesses.

My living example for this is the extent to which Kevin Roberts and I have been a duo at Saatchi & Saatchi for over a decade. When we were a stand-alone, British-based PLC, I was the Executive Chairman and Kevin was the Chief Executive. I did all the "public company stuff," and he delivered all the "ideas and creative work." I managed the Board and dealt with our accountants, lawyers, bankers, and investors. He dealt with our valued clients and employees in the worldwide organization.

We both shared the same vision for the company. We each knew exactly what we had to do. We kept each other informed, supported each other's needs, and to the organization, we were always one voice.

After we sold the company to Publicis Groupe, Kevin became the sole Chief Executive Worldwide, and I assumed the nonexecutive Chairman role. I offer "advice, counsel, and perspective" by saying what I think based on my experience; and people can choose whether to follow it. In Kevin's case, sometimes he does, sometimes he doesn't, but he always listens.

Additionally, I can say or write things to him that might be difficult for others simply because I have no future personal expectations in the company. Sometimes in meetings, I take the pressure off Kevin by saying what obviously needs to be said even though the message might contain a negative observation. I also know when to be silent.

BOB'S WISDOM: Two heads are better than one, and they work optimally when there is a clear understanding of the relative roles and responsibilities of the individuals involved.

The Art and Science of
Selecting the Chief Executive Officer

There is no task for a company more important than selecting the Chief Executive Officer. A company can have only one leader, and if the person is not right for the role, it can all go downhill quickly.

Having witnessed good and not-so-good choices of CEOs in several settings, I have come to the conclusion that making the right selection is both art and science. The best article I have read on the subject was written by Harry Levinson. It was entitled, "Criteria for Choosing Chief Executives," and it appeared in the July–August 1980 edition of the *Harvard Business Review*. Harry Levinson is a psychologist and the founder of the Levinson Institute.

I have used this article countless times for self-evaluations and for assessing people. Each time, I have found it to be highly correlated with success on the job.

In the article, Levinson lists twenty dimensions of personality that he found to be most important most frequently, as well as a scale of characteristics to use in evaluating behavior against the dimensions. The dimensions fall into three categories: Thinking; Feelings and Interrelationships; and Outward Behavior Characteristics.

The following chart shows the five dimensions (numbered as they appeared in the article) that I consider to be most important, arrayed against the last two of what Levinson lists as five scales for evaluation.

Thinking	Scale	⟶▷
1. Capacity to abstract, to conceptualize, to organize, and to integrate different data into a coherent frame of reference.	Can criticize theory and use it for long-range thinking about business.	Encyclopedic synthesis; able to organize and integrate creatively principles, values, concepts, and information from full range of arts and sciences.
4. Judgment, knows when to act.	Good judgment, usually sees whole picture, but has blind spots in some areas.	Excellent judgment, very few mistakes over the years.

Feelings and Interrelationships	Scale	⟶▷
6. Takes a vigorous orientation to problems and needs of the organization.	Attacks problems tactically from new positions and consolidates forces. Subordinates willing to follow.	Attacks problem strategically, with well-defined targets. Plans long-term, step-by-step inexorable advance ahead of competition.
12. Articulateness, makes a good impression.	Handles himself or herself well in public, but has difficulty dealing with hostile questions and unfriendly audiences.	Extremely presentable, has a wide-ranging vocabulary. Inspires audience confidence, senses audience moods. Respected by peers for verbalizing and presenting their problems.

Outward behavior Characteristics	Scale	⟶▷
16. Vision, is clear about progression of his or her own life and career.	Well-defined goals, but behavior suggests that the personal agenda, for which organization is a device, is paramount.	Well-defined goals, consistent with organization's needs and values, consistently pursued.

The dimensions listed on the left-hand side all are critically important for a CEO. The evaluative characteristics on the right-hand scale are discerning in character. The differences as you move from left to right can be quite striking.

In my experience, the people who qualify for the Chief Executive's chair need to be all the way to the right of the evaluative scale on 85% of all twenty dimensions.

As you use this tool to sort out CEO aspirants, you obviously complement it with their track record of accomplishments. This is likely to be at a high level for all candidates. The most discriminating analysis may well be their personality profiles against the dimensions most associated with CEO requirements. Personality runs deep and is not easy to change.

BOB'S WISDOM: Organizations run on leadership, starting with the CEO. Be very deliberate about the qualities you seek.

Evaluating High Performers

My primary technique for evaluating someone's performance is what I call "Footprints in the Snow." These are the distinctive results from a particular person's presence in a situation or environment that probably would not have happened, or certainly would not have happened as well, had that person not been there. They are achievements that are above and beyond a high level of ongoing performance and represent a track record of distinguished accomplishments.

All successful people inevitably leave footprints behind them. They do not have to be great in number, but they must be important. To not leave footprints is a sign of weak performance.

The following is a personal example of the footprints evaluation technique. When I joined Cordiant as Chief Executive, the company was in chaos. The Saatchi brothers had departed, the company had too much debt, and clients and staff were asking whether they should stay or leave. At the end of my first five years, I had made five major footprints in the company:

1. Stabilizing clients and staff
2. Refinancing the company
3. Strategizing and executing a demerger
4. Hiring an exceptional and successful CEO as my successor
5. Leading a highly successful merger with Publicis Groupe.

They averaged out to be one big accomplishment per year.

As indicated, one of my footprints at Saatchi & Saatchi was hiring Kevin Roberts as my successor and CEO Worldwide. On the occasion of his tenth anniversary with the company, I sent him a letter congratulating him on this milestone and cited ten of his remarkable footprints. They focused on distinctive revenue enhancements, organization building, thought leadership, and securing new business. Interestingly enough, Kevin's footprints also averaged one big accomplishment per year.

.

BOB'S WISDOM: High performers are identified by their "Footprints in the Snow." The bigger and more distinctive they are, the greater the impact the person is having.

Evaluating the Chief Executive Officer

As Executive Chairman of Saatchi & Saatchi, it was my responsibility to evaluate the Chief Executive and communicate this to the Board of Directors. In order to provide more than just a personal assessment, I used two published frameworks. The first was "Guidelines for CEO Performance" published by the National Association of Corporate Directors. The second was an article published in the June 21, 1999, issue of *Fortune* magazine describing the characteristics of failed versus superior CEOs. I used the superior CEO framework for my evaluation.

The National Association of Corporate Directors suggests eight areas for review:

1. Leadership
2. Strategic planning
3. Financial results
4. Succession planning
5. Human resources
6. Communications
7. External relations
8. Board relations

My view is that leadership, financial results, communications, and external relations are the most important.

The Chief Executive Officer is the leader of the organization. Without exceptional leadership, there is no team. This is the first prerequisite for a CEO. The second is financial results because for a highly successful CEO, "the buck stops here" is a literal assertion. Investors are not interested in explanations; they require solutions and results. The third criterion is communications. This must be done superbly internally so as to rally the organization. It must be done superbly externally so as to gain the recognition and support that the company deserves. To the public, the CEO *is* the company.

The *Fortune* article listed the following characteristics associated with superior CEOs:

1. Integrity, maturity, and energy
2. Business acumen
3. People acumen
4. Organizational acumen
5. Curiosity, intellectual capacity, and a global mindset
6. Superior judgment
7. An insatiable appetite for accomplishment and results
8. Powerful motivation to grow and convert learning into practice

Of these eight, the last four are the most important. The first four are "club dues."

Curiosity, intellectual capacity, and a global mindset represent three great fundamentals for a CEO. I particularly like intellectual capacity as a starting point. There is nothing like great brainpower as a discriminating asset. To be a successful CEO, however, it must be complemented by other attributes. Brains alone do not get you there.

Superior judgment complements intellectual capacity, particularly when it combines experience, exposure, common sense, and street smarts.

An insatiable appetite for accomplishment and results is important because such is the lot of a CEO. It is a "what have you done for me lately" kind of job. Remember, the DNA of investors is impatience.

Finally, a powerful motivation to grow and convert learning into practice is important because a CEO must be attuned to changing times, ready to adapt quickly, and bravely lead his organization into the new world as it emerges each day. Adaptability and flexibility are necessary characteristics.

There are two other characteristics that a superior CEO requires. The first is the ability to integrate multifunctional inputs for the benefit of the company. The CEO's office is indeed the place where it "all comes together."

The second is optimism—seeing opportunity and advantage where no one else does, and seizing it to make the company a winner. Most people prefer to be part of a successful company rather than a middling or failing one. Being the optimist in business is to be brutally realistic yet determined to surpass obstacles. Every organization has bands of optimists who can manage risks and optimize results. It is the Chief Executive's job to unleash this energy.

BOB'S WISDOM: Evaluating the CEO is a multifaceted task. With leadership beginning at the top, the CEO must be the highest performer in the company.

What Winners Learn from Losing

Red Auerbach and Woody Hayes were winners, but even the best of us face an occasional defeat. The key questions are, "How are you going to handle it?" and "Where do you go from there?" Red and Woody offered the following insights:

Red Auerbach said, "People who always look for reasons why they do not win create the effect of making it acceptable and easy to lose."

And Woody Hayes' advice was: "Look for a cleansing effect when you get beaten."

Red was concerned about people making excuses and blaming defeat on outside forces such as the referees, the fans, or the travel schedule. To him, these factors were always present for both sides, so he never made excuses. He just said, "We got beaten," and then went about correcting the problem.

A similar phenomenon exists in business. There are those people who spend a lot of time explaining the reasons for their poor performance. As long as they have an explanation, they seem to feel that performing below expectations is acceptable.

In contrast, there are others who react to below-plan performance by identifying underlying causes and proposing solutions to get back on plan. Give me the latter group, and do not send me the former bunch!

The group that is on the initiative in proposing solutions to get back on plan is made up of the people who will ultimately be winners.

Woody viewed losing like a shock to the system. He hated to lose, and when it happened, it meant that something was wrong and had to be identified, dealt with, and corrected.

Again, so it is in business. When things are not going well, until you get the truth out on the table, no matter how ugly, you are not in a position to deal with it. One of the things I try to do as a Chairman is to ensure that we start with an open, honest, and candid assessment of the situation, and then go on from there. That is the way you achieve what Woody would call a "cleansing effect."

BOB'S WISDOM: Do not look for excuses when you underperform. Look for underlying reasons so you can avoid doing it again.

Occupy the High Ground

When General Foods transferred me to Washington, D.C. in 1970 as a District Sales Manager, we knew we would be living in the area for a limited time, so Sarah and I used to pack our sons into the car every weekend and go on a sightseeing expedition.

One of our favorite pastimes was visiting Civil War battle sites—Bull Run, Fredericksburg, Antietam, and Gettysburg. I am not a military man, but one of the things you learn about when you visit these battle sites is the principle of "occupy the high ground."

This applies in business, too. Except, it is most often the moral high ground as exemplified by sound principles, values, and beliefs that ultimately wins the day. In an era of corporate dishonesty such as we have seen with Enron and WorldCom, this might not always seem to be the case. But history will show that these companies represent negative blips and their practices are not seen as the basis for long-term success.

The principle was driven home to me at Saatchi & Saatchi on Valentine's Day 2005. We had a walkout of personnel from our New York office who thought they could leave us, take a very important client over to another agency, and personally benefit from the whole affair. It would not have been the first time in the history of advertising that such a situation occurred, and the popular press set about predicting this scenario would likely be the case for us. As it turned out, it was not the case at all—not even close.

Saatchi & Saatchi prevailed with the client, and they remain with us to this day. The simple reason for this, beyond the fact that we had a long-term relationship and had done great work, was that in this situation we occupied the moral high ground. The client demonstrated the utmost integrity and recognized that we had no hand in causing this state of affairs. Both we and they would have been the victims of someone's self-interest that clearly could not have worked to the client's long-term advantage, and they did not permit it to occur.

BOB'S WISDOM: Build your business relationships on integrity supported by sound principles, values, and beliefs.

You Get What You Expect

Another important point Woody Hayes made to our group at General Foods was "Expect a lot from your people. They will meet it." For Woody, this meant that each new team would follow in the tradition of a long line of winners. They would expect to have a winning season, expect to win the Big Ten championship, expect to go to the Rose Bowl, and expect to contend for the national title.

To help him set these expectations, Woody had on film the greatest plays from his greatest teams. Picture yourself as a rookie running back in a team meeting. The film comes on and Woody is narrating, saying things like, "Watch this run. This is one of the greatest runs of all time. That's Hop-a-long Cassidy. He was a Heisman Trophy winner. You can run like that. You can do that, too."

With this inspiration and encouragement, set against an expectation of individuals working toward personal and team goals of peak performance, Woody designed the practices and coaching sessions to bring out the best in every player.

Apparently, the technique worked pretty well because he coached 56 All-Americans, including three Heisman Trophy winners.

Woody's words inspired me to deliver one of the finest talks I ever gave. It was to the Maxwell House Division Management Council, a forum of the top 75 or so people in the division drawn from all functional areas. We gathered this group together several times a year to review business results, strategies, upcoming plans, and overall expectations. Our vision was to be the "Best Coffee Company."

I ended my remarks by unveiling a token remembrance of the meeting. It was a "Best Coffee Company" mirror with the Maxwell House logo. I asked each person to hang theirs in a prominent place, either at home or in their office, look in it at the end of every day and ask themselves, "What did I do today to help Maxwell House become the Best Coffee Company?" If the answer was "nothing," then they had a lot of work to do tomorrow.

This simple device told everyone that they were important, needed to be accountable, and that they should reflect on what they personally were doing every day to help make us the best.

BOB'S WISDOM: Set an expectation for your people to be the best they can be at what they do, and ensure they have everything they need to make it happen.

"Don't Tell, Ask"

Two sporting legends who met with us at General Foods provided overlapping advice. Red Auerbach said, "Don't tell people to do things, ask them." Jack Twyman went even further when he said, "Don't ask things of others that you are not prepared to do yourself."

This advice certainly is relevant to me in my current job offering advice, counsel, and perspective. I do not "tell" people anything. I ask that they listen to what I have to say and then decide what to do on their own.

The Auerbach-Twyman principles also apply to line operating executives. You cannot get the job done alone, so you need to delegate responsibilities and people need to stand up and be accountable for their actions. They are a lot more likely to respond in a positive way if you ask, rather than tell them what you want done.

At the same time, applying the Twyman principle of "Don't ask things of others that you are not prepared to do yourself" certainly increases the legitimacy of your requests.

To illustrate, in August 1976, I became the Strategic Business Unit Manager for Beverages at General Foods. I wasn't there at the inception of the idea, but during my tenure, we introduced Country Time powdered lemonade drink nationwide. It was an instant success. On a hot day in the middle of the summer, there is nothing that quenches your thirst quite like a cold glass of lemonade. So, Country Time met a real, albeit seasonal, consumer need.

Several years later, I returned to the Beverage Division as the head of the Packaged Convenience Foods Sector. In the interim, following the recommendation of a consulting organization, the company had installed a classification system for its brands. Class I was "Grow." Class II was "Maintain." Class III was "Harvest." I was never a fan of the classification system. My belief was that you had to have an attitude of growing all the brands in the businesses. Words like "Maintain" and "Harvest" in our business were slippery slopes indeed.

At any rate, I called a meeting to review the Beverage business and was told by a new-to-the-brand product manager that Country Time had been placed in Class III—Harvest. I could not believe my ears! There was no truly competitive alternative lemonade-flavored powdered drink, and there was still nothing more thirst-quenching on a hot summer's day.

I did not accept the product manager's rationale, and asked that Country Time be supported and grown. He then began to tell me all the reasons this should not be done. I said, "Fine, I will peel Country Time out of the Division, get a brand manager, and do it myself in my spare time" (of which I had none).

Now the meeting really went topsy-turvy. The thought of a Group Vice-President running a brand as a sideline out of his office was a little too much. Division managers started to fall all over themselves to volunteer for the task, but it was only because they realized I was deadly serious and that I would do it myself.

You know what? Country Time was relaunched with great success, and as a corollary, I made a significant statement about the importance of growth and common sense with the group.

BOB'S WISDOM: Asking people to do what they know you are prepared to do yourself can be transformative.

To Try and to Succeed

In the Packaged Convenience Foods Sector at General Foods, there were four operating divisions—Beverages, Desserts, Main Meals, and Birds-Eye frozen foods. I entered the business at a point when annual revenues exceeded $2.5 billion, but growth had stagnated and profits were suffering as a result.

I called a staff meeting and passed out three pieces of paper to each Division head. The first piece said, "To Try and To Succeed." The second piece said, "To Try and To Fail." The third piece said, "To Not Try, and therefore, Not Fail."

Since we probably could all agree that the first piece of paper was the most highly valued, I wanted to know which of the remaining two pieces was most highly valued in their divisions. To my amazement and chagrin, the majority said "To Not Try, and therefore, Not Fail." Now, I knew we had a big problem.

To be successful in business, you have to accept that periodic failure of a good effort is part of the deal. You cannot punish failure. Indeed, you have to prize it as part of the learning and development process. This is the only way that you can ultimately get the first and most highly valued piece of paper—"To Try and To Succeed."

We put things back on track in Packaged Convenience Foods by making it clear that we considered growth to be mandatory, and viewed periodic failure simply as a valued by-product of trying and succeeding.

BOB'S WISDOM: Make sure that fear of failure is not keeping your organization from trying and succeeding.

Delegation: The Art of Letting Go and Holding On

As your career advances, your responsibilities expand and you grow increasingly dependent on others to get the job done. You become the person who sets directions and, while you may be the approver for major initiatives, the talent to lead the myriad activities required for excellence in execution and producing good results lies within the organization. Accordingly, it is important to think carefully about how and to whom you assign accountabilities.

From the outset, you should consider various principles. The first one is clarity. Accountabilities should be absolutely clear to the person involved as well as to the organization at large. That way everyone knows who is responsible and is therefore, the "go to" person.

A second principle to consider is focus. For every activity or assignment that is truly important, I like to have someone who essentially spends all of their time on that task. That way there can be no finger-pointing or passing of the buck.

A third consideration is scope. In my experience, it is important not to spread people too thinly. Highly motivated individuals usually want increased responsibilities, but if the proper support structures are not in place, this can become a self-fulfilling prophecy for failure. The unfortunate person ends up doing one thing well at the expense of another project being poorly executed.

Something I am always wary of, is what people call "shared accountabilities." This is usually a formula for management by committee, an approach where no one is actually in charge.

Another reason clearly assigned accountabilities are important is that they represent the basis for evaluating, recognizing, and rewarding people. Without this clarity, it is difficult to determine salary actions and the basis for promotions.

I have a test for whether we have clearly assigned accountabilities in the organization. When I go to bed at night, I like to be able to name the clearly accountable person for all the important projects going on. If I can do this, I fall asleep right away. If I cannot, it means I will have a sleepless night thinking about how to get it fixed as soon as possible.

BOB'S WISDOM: As your own responsibilities expand, clearly assigning accountabilities is the way to get things done.

How Leaders Should Be
Involved in Decision Making

Most organizations have approval levels that usually require the head person to be the approver on major projects. If you are that person, all significant decisions ultimately will pass by your desk. But be aware, waiting around for this stage in the process leaves you in the position of "take it or leave it," and it does not adequately use you as a resource.

I prefer to be involved at three stages. The first is at the inception of the idea. Becoming involved at this point gives me the opportunity to get the idea up on my radar screen, to make sure that the breadth of exploration will be broad enough, and to ensure that it is being properly resourced. During this stage, the organization goes to work exploring a range of alternatives for bringing the idea to fruition.

The second stage at which I want to be involved is what I call the "winnowing down" stage, the point at which most alternatives are discarded and the team begins to focus in on a single course of action. This is the most important stage in decision making because it is the time when I can understand the pros and cons of all the alternatives and make sure the right choices are being made. Once this stage is passed, the organization's efforts should be fully focused on the chosen alternative.

The final stage—approval—should take place naturally and smoothly if everyone was in agreement at stage two. The emphasis in the final approval meeting need not be on the strategic choice, but on excellence in execution.

BOB'S WISDOM: Do not wait around for the "take it or leave it" approval stage in decision making. Focus your involvement in ways that maximize your ability to be a resource.

Go Home and Sleep Like a Baby

Running an international enterprise is a demanding task. You are based at headquarters and your units are scattered all over the world. You periodically visit them to see what is going on firsthand, but inevitably these turn out to be programmed events. Everyone knows you are coming, an agenda is established, and they all work hard to impress.

More often than not, things go pretty well while you are on site. The local staff have worked overtime in preparation (there may even be fresh paint on the walls). How then do you make an assessment of the real state of affairs?

I have found two things to be useful. First, you need to mandate a format for any business review that ensures you can clearly appraise the facts of the situation. I like to see results for the current year in the context of three years of history, and I require that any reviews include external measures such as market trends, share of market, and competitor results.

Second, as I am waving goodbye to the management team, I ask myself the same question at the end of every visit. It goes like this, "I have been here for 2–3 days. Things went well, but during the other 362 days of the year, what happens here will be in the hands of the people that I am now waving goodbye to. Do I have confidence that they are the team that will carry us to victory?"

If the answer to the question is "Yes" then I can fly home and sleep like a baby. If the answer is "No" then sleepless nights await me until I put in place a team that I have confidence in.

BOB'S WISDOM: On site visits, review the facts to validate your confidence in the management team. If things aren't right, make changes.

Sometimes You Have to Fire People

During my tenure at General Foods, I had three off-campus staff meetings featuring guest speakers from the world of sports who had become legends in their own time—Woody Hayes, Red Auerbach, and Jack Twyman.

The premise was that as winners, these men had values, beliefs, and principles that could be transferred to our world of business. Individually, they had wise advice on many subjects. But on one topic in particular, they were unanimous—to build a great team, you must select people with care and decisively remove those who do not make the grade.

Woody Hayes: "Kick off players that do not perform."
Red Auerbach: "Don't let things fester—they'll multiply."
Jack Twyman: "Have the right team. If someone does not fit, get rid of them."

Woody was so good at selection, that he only had to "kick off" three players in 28 years.

One of my greatest errors in personnel management was neglecting to terminate the employment of a person whom I had inherited, but who obviously was not working out. He was not a good team player, nor did he exemplify the values, beliefs, and principles I stood for. I did not take immediate action because of his substantial termination allowance, which I felt was inappropriate. I wasted two years before he finally departed. In hindsight, it would have been better to pay the money and build a strong and complete team from the beginning.

I learned a serious lesson that I later applied in another case where I participated in what turned out to be a poor hiring decision that became apparent in the first five months. This time, I swallowed my pride and terminated the individual's employment during month six. Sure, it was embarrassing to have to reverse course in such a short period, but it cleared the deck toward a productive future, both for the company and, fortunately, for the individual involved. Like Red, I did not let things fester.

When the time comes to terminate an individual's employment, there is always the question of approach. These individuals usually know they are in a problem situation. My stance is to be candid and act decisively and fairly by fully concluding any contractual obligations, including severance pay, and when appropriate, offering outplacement services.

BOB'S WISDOM: Select your team members carefully, and act decisively and fairly when terminating their employment.

Left-Brained Management of Right-Brained People

I was an international consumer packaged goods management person on the client side for twenty-eight years before becoming involved with Saatchi & Saatchi via Cordiant in 1995.

Saatchi & Saatchi is one of the most creative companies in the world. We consistently rank in the top three at the annual Cannes Advertising Festival. In 2007 our New York agency won "Agency of the Year" at Cannes. Local winners of this accolade have gone to Saatchi & Saatchi in countries from Argentina, Australia, Brazil, Costa Rica, and Denmark to New Zealand, Poland, Singapore, and Slovakia. The "Every Day Matters" campaign for JCPenney won "Marketing Campaign of the Year" at the World Retail Awards in 2008.

When I first joined the company, I used to get calls from my old client friends who would ask in a somewhat bewildered tone, "How in the world do you deal with all those creative people?" The answer is relatively straightforward if you pursue certain principles. Here is how I do it.

First, from my client background I have a keen appreciation for why companies hire an advertising agency in the first place—to get access to right-brained creative people who bring consumer insights, ideas, and strategic communications that we left-brained clients could never generate on our own—all to increase sales.

Second, I have an appreciation of left/right side of the brain considerations because my wife wrote her Master of Education thesis on the subject of laterality of the brain. As a result, I arrived at a top creative company with my eyes wide open.

Like most professionals, creative people want to be in an environment that highly values their work. At Saatchi & Saatchi, our

Inspirational Dream begins with "To be revered as the hothouse for world-changing creative ideas." This statement was written by our Worldwide Creative Board. It is what we are all about and it is the kind of environment that creative people relish being a part of.

Once on board, they want to be free to practice their craft. They revel in their work. It's not a factory process. No one should ever think that creativity is easy. Creative people invest a vast amount of emotion and brainpower in their ideas, and giving birth to them is said to be a bit like having children. At Saatchi & Saatchi we try to operate in the most hassle-free manner we possibly can. There are many principles that we all share, and we don't have a lot of oppressive processes and procedures.

Creative people want to be supported by their management. They know what they are good at, and they frequently understand their limits as well. Sometimes we left-brainers can take the heat off what would be a tough situation for a right-brained individual simply by relieving pressure and reducing tension.

Creative people like to be recognized and loved. I suppose we all like this, but creative people seem to thrive on an extra quotient of love. They also like winning awards, so we compete aggressively for the world's top advertising awards to gain recognition for the work of our creative teams.

Overall, in contrast to what my bewildered callers sometimes ask, my own feeling is that creative people are easy to unleash. You just have to focus on the right triggers.

BOB'S WISDOM: Creative people first and foremost want to be valued, supported, recognized, and loved in an environment that lets them practice their craft.

The Chief Executive Officer's Obligation

One of the first obligations of the Chief Executive Officer is to ensure the perpetuation of the firm. I was reminded of this when Philip Morris took ownership of General Foods in 1985.

In the months preceding the actual event, there had been much speculation in the press about Philip Morris acquiring a food company. Their primary rival at the time, R.J. Reynolds, had acquired Nabisco, and many observers felt that this event alone would propel Philip Morris into action.

When I inquired of my boss at General Foods as to what might be going on, he said, "You just focus on the business. We have formed a group that is looking at this. Don't worry." I spoke to a finance person who was a member of that group, and he told me that he believed no offer would be forthcoming. He indicated that his staff had run the acquisition parameters through the General Foods return on investment criteria and they had fallen well short of the minimum hurdle rate. This led him to conclude that Philip Morris would not act.

That prophecy, of course, was not to be. Philip Morris initiated a tender offer for General Foods and the multibillion-dollar takeover, the largest in U.S. corporate history outside of the oil industry at the time, was concluded shortly thereafter.

Philip Morris was most gracious in the aftermath, and invited a cadre of General Foods management personnel from White Plains down to their New York City headquarters to discuss what had transpired.

I recall Hamish Maxwell, the Chairman and CEO of Philip Morris at the time, holding up a copy of *Fortune* magazine from the 1950s and citing a number of leading organizations, including steel companies and meatpacking companies that had since fallen by the wayside. He remarked, "It was my job never to allow that to happen to Philip Morris." Accordingly, he had used their huge cash flow to diversify their capital assets and thereby perpetuate the firm.

I subsequently talked with a strategic planning manager at Philip Morris who indicated that they had never run the return on investment calculation that the General Foods finance person had taken solace in. Rather, they had the cash, they could afford it, and the acquisition was not dilutive to earnings per share. Simply put, they saw the whole situation through a totally different lens. Their primary motivation had been to perpetuate the firm.

BOB'S WISDOM: Ensure perpetuation of the firm by staying in touch with the world around you and constantly looking about and ahead.

SECTION SEVEN

Building Culture through Communications

One Team, One Dream

One of the slogans we added to the language at Saatchi & Saatchi was "One Team, One Dream." Actually, Kevin Roberts first heard these words when he was doing research for the book, *Peak Performance* (New York: Harper Collins, 2000). The line was uttered by none other than Michael Jordan about the spirit of the Chicago Bulls.

We borrowed it at Saatchi & Saatchi as a complement to "Nothing Is Impossible." Together, they define our spirit. "Nothing Is Impossible" is a great attitude, but on its own it can also be an excuse for wild, reckless behavior. "One Team, One Dream" harnesses the spirit to be in the best interests of all.

"One Team, One Dream" is a great attitude for a worldwide company to adopt. It encourages our people to work together on behalf of our clients and prevents our many offices and business units from degenerating into a world of fiefdoms and silos.

We make "One Team, One Dream" real via a policy that says no local bonuses get paid unless we deliver our worldwide commitment first. This proves we walk the talk.

BOB'S WISDOM: The people in your company all need to be in the same boat. The philosophy and practice of "One Team, One Dream" makes it actual.

"Breakfast with Bob"

W hen your company is owned by investment bankers and is in a turnaround situation, it is a tense time for the employees. They know that things will be different, it will be a demanding period, and there will be a transaction with attendant uncertainty at the other end of the deal. Such was the environment I faced at Kayser-Roth, which was owned by a joint venture between the Blackstone Group and Wasserstein-Perella.

On my first day with the company, I addressed the entire headquarters group. I introduced myself, offered my perspective on the current situation, and laid out a road map showing how we would proceed. This was a good start, but I wanted to get closer to everyone in the company. Having run a number of different organizations, I knew the best way to learn about an enterprise was to get to know the employees.

So we launched "Breakfast with Bob"—a program whereby I would have breakfast with 400 people, pretty close to every employee at headquarters. At a rate of seven people at a time, twice a week, I met with everyone in only 29 weeks. Given that most people had never even met the President and CEO, let alone have a one-hour breakfast with him, it was unprecedented.

It gave me an opportunity to learn a lot about the company, to create an open dialogue that broke down barriers, and to put on the table what we needed to do together.

I had to vary the format each time because people would chat with their peers about what happened at these sessions, but the general thrust went like this. We opened by going around the table, introducing ourselves, explaining what we did, how long we had been with the company, and telling a story about our personal lives. I always started it off. On the personal side, I'd usually talk about my wife, our three sons, our pet cat, or our interests in travel and gardening.

We all had pads and pencils and I would ask three questions, giving people time to make notes regarding their thoughts and responses. After getting breakfast from the cafeteria line, we would come back and talk about them.

The best three questions were:

1. "What do you like most about the company?"
2. "What is the single most important thing you would like to see us change?"
3. "What is the one thing we could do differently that would help you to do your job better?"

I would ask for a volunteer to start and move the discussion along through all three topics ensuring that we got everyone to participate.

I learned that the employees really liked working at Kayser-Roth. They were proud of the quality products the company manufactured. Recently, however, they had been poorly led, there had been many shifts in strategy, and there was a general inability to achieve excellence in execution. People knew the company had to change, and they were up for it. All they asked was for the leadership to set the company in the right direction and then see it through.

Most of the ideas for improvement centered on the need to improve communications, reduce bureaucracy, and increase speed of decision making.

We ended these sessions with me giving the group an opportunity to ask anything they wanted about me, about the company, about the owners, or anything at all. I even got the inevitable, "boxers or briefs?" The most frequently asked questions centered on the implications of investment bank ownership and what was likely to happen. I answered every question as best as I could.

At the end, each participant was given a "Bob Had Breakfast with Me" coffee mug. Seven months later, everyone in the company had one.

This organization-wide activity created an environment where every employee felt like a valued colleague who was being asked to contribute to and be part of the solutions we needed to become a successful company. It broke down boundaries, cut through layers, and built an open dialogue.

BOB'S WISDOM: Every person in your organization is important to its success. When you're the leader, spend quality time with your people to stay connected.

Ability + Chemistry = Team

When describing how he built nine Boston Celtic NBA title-winning teams, Red Auerbach said, "The first thing is ability; the second is chemistry."

On the one hand, he had to recruit top players and on the other hand, he had to know how to blend them into a winning team. Let's consider some of his top players.

Bill Russell may not have had the individual stats of Wilt Chamberlain, but he was a team player and a true winner. John Havlicek probably was not the most individually brilliant player of his time, but he was the one player that every coach would have liked to build his team around for the long term. And fortunately for Red, Larry Bird had the distinction of being both the best individual player and the best team player of his day.

In a marketing-driven manufacturing organization, your supporting functional resource managers must not only be good at managing their function, but also be capable of doing it from a marketing point of view.

Your operations manager needs to accept that consumers demand multiple sizes and retailers expect certain levels of turnover, even though the plant would run more efficiently if there were fewer sizes and case packs.

Your logistics manager needs to understand that consistently meeting the high order delivery standards of a Wal-Mart is a precondition to being in distribution and having your company considered as an integral promotional partner. And your research manager needs to accept that a technology is only relevant if it results in increased consumer satisfaction.

This may all sound obvious and routine. In my experience, it is not. To be functionally excellent as well as marketing empathetic is a demanding combination that not all people, even the truly talented ones, have in sufficient quantities.

Then there is the chemistry part. The first person your staff has to have chemistry with is you. This requires an open door, an ongoing dialogue, and lots of one-on-one time. I employed all these tools, plus I would periodically go for a long lunch or dinner out of the office to build relationships.

Regular staff meetings are an obvious way to build the team as you manage the business together. The frequency of these meetings varies according to circumstances. When I was a Division Manager, I had them weekly. When I was a Multi-division Manager, I had them monthly. At Saatchi & Saatchi, we convene our Worldwide Executive Board three times a year.

Another tool for building the chemistry of the team are off-campus staff meetings in desirable but sensible locations, built around stimulating themes, and sometimes featuring guest speakers. In a worldwide organization, hosting meetings in various parts of the world exposes the staff to different business environments and allows management to "show the flag" at the same time we are building the team.

I took my Kayser-Roth executive staff to the Center for Creative Leadership in North Carolina with the specific mission of all taking the Myers-Briggs test to better understand who we were individually and how we complemented each other.

At Saatchi & Saatchi, we employ "purposing" sessions taken from the *Peak Performance* book to help build our teams and ensure that they are all moving forward in the same direction. These are very involving sessions that get us to the best answers while consolidating our teamwork in the process.

BOB'S WISDOM: Building a great team requires getting the right talent and then blending them to achieve the right chemistry.

Nothing Is Impossible

"Nothing Is Impossible" has been the mantra of Saatchi & Saatchi since its inception. Perhaps it was an inevitable phrase for the two sons of Iraqi parents who emigrated to London in 1947 and built what arguably is the most famous name in advertising. Or, perhaps it was an early signal that in 1994, the brothers might reach too far, and it would all fall away from them.

Whatever its origins, these three incredibly powerful words— "Nothing Is Impossible"—have defined the attitude and spirit of 7,000 people around the globe every day of every year for more than three decades. One could not have chosen three words more wisely.

Nothing Is Impossible says no challenge is too great, no task is too large—we can do anything. It matters not what the odds are—we can overcome them. You tell us the problem—we will generate a solution. It leads us to think out of the box, the square, the circle, and consistently entertain unconventional thinking. It causes us to welcome change— because we know we can bend its edge to our advantage.

Nothing Is Impossible is timeless, and for the people at Saatchi & Saatchi, it is our way of life.

Adopting a mantra for your company can be a powerful tool. Nike did it with "Just Do It." Procter & Gamble is doing it with "The Consumer Is Boss"—a great attitude for a consumer packaged goods company. Finding a mantra that really works for an organization is a challenging task. It needs to be short, sweet, meaningful, relevant, and timeless.

BOB'S WISDOM: Mantras are powerful tools for uniting and directing the attitudes of your people, clients, and customers. Choose one wisely because it can serve you for decades.

Passionate, Competitive, Restless

The Saatchi brothers had three criteria for hiring people. Candidates had to be passionate, competitive, and restless. These are the characteristics that we continue to look for in employees around the world today.

Our business is hard work. It is fast-moving, intense, demanding, and pressure-packed, entails hard deadlines, and usually is on the cutting edge of change. If you are going to perform in the advertising industry, you have to love what you do. That is where passion comes in. We like to hire people who would not want to be anywhere else and really love the rather crazy jobs they do.

Our people also need to be competitive on behalf of our company and on behalf of our clients. We want winners who will fight hard for new business versus other agencies and consultancies, and who identify with and fight for our clients in their competitive arenas. Winning share of market is a constant measure of our progress. We also compete aggressively for the top international and national advertising awards.

Our people need to be restless and edgy, with a healthy dissatisfaction for the status quo. They must subscribe to the notion that Nothing Is Impossible. We must be constantly innovating new ideas because an idea is original only once. We need foresight, not hindsight. Being constantly restless keeps us on the winning edge in our business.

BOB'S WISDOM: Passionate, competitive, and restless are three key characteristics of the people in successful creative companies.

Be Relentless, Be Relentless

"Relentless" is a strong and powerful word. It represents effective behavior in getting things done, particularly when it describes an unyielding and passionate attitude toward core values that our people really care about; values that are universal in their application and timeless in character.

Saatchi & Saatchi has an agency called Team One in Los Angeles that develops all the advertising for Toyota's Lexus. Eighteen years ago, they developed an end line for Lexus commercials that said, "The Relentless Pursuit of Perfection." This line captured the core tenet of Lexus engineering as expressed by the Japanese word *Kaizen*, which means "continuous improvement." The Lexus philosophy demands that they make nearly every aspect of every car better than the previous one, every time. This means not only continuously challenging their own company standards but reinventing and surpassing industry standards as well. It extends to customer service in addition to being applied to manufacturing. This relentless behavior has produced incredible business results. In 2007, they sold approximately 320,000 vehicles in the United States, up 400 percent compared with 10 years ago. In a brutally tough U.S. market, Lexus finished #1 in luxury sales in 2008.

Kevin Roberts has been relentless in establishing Lovemarks as a new concept in marketing. When he first introduced the idea in 2000, there were skeptics both within the company and in the business world at large. Kevin stayed with it, refining and reinforcing it. To date, it has spawned significant new business, a book series and indeed, an entirely new way of approaching communications. Lovemarks is an idea that never went away because Kevin was relentless in his pursuit of bringing it to life.

Saatchi & Saatchi can be relentless in its pursuit of Nothing Is Impossible because it is timeless in character. Each new addition to its litany of Nothing Is Impossible success stories contributes to its endurance as a corporate philosophy.

Procter & Gamble can be relentless in its pursuit of "The Consumer Is Boss" because it is universal in application to their business. Meeting consumer needs is at the core of what the company is all about.

I am relentless about always starting with an open, honest, and candid assessment of the facts, as it consistently represents the best starting point for dealing with a situation.

You must learn to be relentless about the pearls of wisdom that you develop for yourself, because they will become the essence of what you stand for.

BOB'S WISDOM: Be relentless in pursuit of things you are passionate about.

I Can't Say Too Much about Communications

R ed Auerbach and Woody Hayes had some important words about communications.

> Red Auerbach: "Communication is the key to your job. Not just telling people what you require, but rather, making sure they understand."
> Woody Hayes: "Check vertical communications down the line, and all the way through execution."

Red Auerbach had the right advice for a business leader. If you want to lead, your ability to communicate is the key vehicle available for inspiring the people in the organization. The first thing I have done every time I moved to a new situation is to get myself out in front of as many people as possible, letting them know who I am, where I am coming from, and how we plan to proceed. There is no substitute for face time.

The second part of Red's advice is more subtle and important. You cannot just rely on "talk at you" sessions. This may get you started, but there is no guarantee that your audience understands your messages.

The other practice I employ in new situations is to have an extended dinner with each member of my executive staff, not only to get to know them and hear them out, but to ensure they understand me and how I like to work.

Off-campus staff meetings are another tool for generating an extensive uninterrupted discussion of matters that can help create understanding. At Kayser-Roth, I employed forums like "K-R Live" and "Breakfast with Bob" to broaden and deepen my interpersonal communications.

Woody Hayes' comment about checking vertical communications down the line, is an important complement to Red Auerbach's advice.

Woody knew that it is one thing to say something. It is another to ensure that it is being understood and executed properly.

That is why you have to get out in the field and to plant locations and check on the interpretation of headquarters' directions. I learned early on as a District Manager that interpretation is not always what headquarters intended. Plus, when you are out in the field or at a plant location, it helps that you are being seen. It shows that you care, and it makes the communication real. Fundamentally, it is hard to over communicate, many opportunities can be lost by under-communicating.

BOB'S WISDOM: Communicate often in a variety of ways, and make sure that what you are saying is understood and properly implemented.

"K-R Live"

Wal-Mart was Kayser-Roth's largest customer. I went to Bentonville, Arkansas, to visit them in 1991, and as part of my visit I was invited to sit in on one of their now famous "Saturday Morning" meetings. It was one of the most energizing and pleasurable sessions I have ever attended.

All the Bentonville employees were convened in a large auditorium, and they began by reviewing business results for the previous week. Then they reviewed what was coming up in the week ahead with emphasis on what it would take to ensure excellence in execution. Talk about management in real time!

People from the audience spontaneously made comments or, in some cases, were called on for input. It was fast-paced, energetic, and upbeat. The inclusive nature made everyone feel they were an important part of the organization, and they certainly all felt and acted like winners.

As I left the meeting, I had two thoughts: "I wonder what the people at Kmart are doing this morning?" and, "How can I apply this experience to my own company?"

I went back to Greensboro and initiated what we called "K-R Live." We were not retailers, so our meeting took place every other Friday morning for no more than an hour. We did not have an auditorium that could fit everyone, so we designated our department heads to attend, and we met in the company cafeteria. Each of them went back to their department and summarized the meeting that day for their teams. Here is the Rules Sheet I passed out at the first session:

The "Kayser-Roth Live" Friday Morning Meeting Rules

Rule 1. Attend.... If You Cannot, Designate Someone From Your Team to Cover

Rule 2. Bring Your Eyes, Ears, and Brain—No Preparation Required Beyond Your Hands-On Knowledge of Your Job or Something You Would Like to Share

Rule 3. Participate.... And/Or, I Will Call On You

Rule 4. Go Back To Your Area and Communicate—Must Host a Department Meeting by Close of Business the Same Day

I developed a talk sheet for these meetings, but we generally focused on results, hot topics, and upcoming events. The meetings dramatically improved our communications and ensured that everyone knew what was going on. More than ever, they felt they were a key part of the corporate team. An important element of a meeting's success was keeping it fast-paced, spontaneous, and with high levels of participation.

BOB'S WISDOM: There is no substitute for frequent and real-time communications to make everyone feel they are part of a winning team.

Repeating a Good Thing Is a Good Thing

When I was a Product Manager, one of my responsibilities was to work with the advertising agency developing media plans. We measured our communications in reach and frequency—how many households did we reach in any given four-week period, and how often did we reach them?

We also employed the concept of "effective reach," which we defined as the need to reach people at least three times in a four-week period if we wanted to communicate our message effectively.

I have continued to keep the concept of effective reach in mind, and translated it into the notion of "never be afraid to repeat a good thing." All too often, people make a point; they think everybody's got it; so they are reluctant to repeat themselves. In truth, the more important the message, the more often you should repeat it, disperse it, and campaign it.

This is particularly applicable to the vision or Inspirational Dream you have for your company. While you may think everyone knows it, the reality is that given employee turnover and growth in a dynamic enterprise, every time you meet with a group, it is likely that 20% of the people are seeing you or hearing you for the first time. Also, hearing directly from you as the leader and being able to sense your conviction helps to drive the message home.

When I travel to various countries for Saatchi & Saatchi, I include our Inspirational Dream in every set of remarks I make to our organizations. It represents the essence of what the company is all about. I also repeated it every time I met with security analysts and investors because this was what they were investing in.

As the Chairman of Saatchi & Saatchi, I spend most of my time dispensing what we call "advice, counsel, and perspective." Inevitably, it is based on the collected bits of wisdom you are reading, as they represent ideas that I have been repeating, and repeating, and repeating for a lifetime.

BOB'S WISDOM: When a message is important, never be afraid to repeat yourself. People rarely get it the first time around.

Coin Your Own "OHCCIMR"

As part of our strategy development at Kayser-Roth, Jane Martin, the manager of our Total Quality Process, asked me what kind of employee environment we wanted to create within the company. I told her that I valued an environment that included open, honest, and candid communications, in an atmosphere characterized by integrity and mutual respect for each other's views. Her response was, "If that is what we want, then we have to tell everyone and make it part of our strategy."

She went off and coined the term *OHCCIMR* (pronounced *ocksimmer*), using the first letter of each of the key words—Open, Honest, Candid Communications, Integrity, and Mutual Respect. We merchandised the term throughout the company via a communications program that let everyone know what we valued.

On the one hand, the whole thing felt a little corny. On the other hand, if something is important, you have to let people know it in language that is universally understood.

There is nothing more important than starting with open, honest, and candid communications, and personally, I cannot abide situations where it is not done with integrity and mutual respect.

BOB'S WISDOM: Let people know what's important to you, and don't be afraid to be a little homespun in the way you do it.

SECTION EIGHT
Personal Style and Spirit

Driving a Ford Fiesta

Sarah and I were married the weekend following our college graduation. We had been the proverbial high school sweethearts and dated
for seven years. Marriage seemed the natural thing to do, and it still feels
the same 40-plus years later!

Our honeymoon was a motor trip through Canada and the New
England states. I had graduated from Harvard College, but with only
eight weeks to go in the summer before starting graduate school, the
highest paying job I could get was as a janitor in the McGraw-Hill
building in Boston. I needed the money so I took it and, consequently,
became somewhat of an expert in cleaning and repairs.

When people received promotions at General Foods, the company
sent announcements to their local newspapers. Our five-year-old son
saw the article reporting my promotion in the Pet Foods Division and
went into school the next day announcing: "My Dad makes dog food"
along with his drawing showing a man stirring a large vat of what was
supposed to be the product. His announcement of my promotion was
far more meaningful than the local newspaper coverage.

In 1982, I was a Group Vice-President for the Packaged Convenience Foods sector when General Foods had the grand opening of its
new "Taj Mahal" corporate headquarters in Rye Brook, New York. Most
of the invited guests came in limousines, but I arrived in my 1979 Ford
Fiesta.

This led one of my son's friends to remark to him, "Gee, I thought
your dad was successful. Why does he drive a Fiesta?"

As Chief Executive at Cordiant in London, my contract included a
car and driver to take me back and forth to work, which I declined and
took the Tube instead. There were not too many Chief Executives of

British-based PLC's riding the Tube, but Green Park to Warren Street was just two stops on the London Underground, and I did not like the idea of someone sitting around, waiting to drive me home.

I mention all of these things only because I think too many executives find themselves operating in a rarefied atmosphere where they begin to lose touch with the real world.

One of the reasons I enjoy success is that I have always been as comfortable talking with people on the factory floor as I am wading into a group of senior executives at a business conference. I have never lost sight of my upbringing in a small New England town, and that I graduated from a public high school where only half of the students went on to college.

BOB'S WISDOM: As you move up the ladder of success, keep yourself grounded and in touch with the real world.

To Improve Your Performance
at Work, Go Home

Striking the right balance between your work and your personal life represents enlightened self-interest when building your career, because an executive bogged down by problems on the home front is unlikely to be a high performer at work, and vice versa.

Building a successful career is a tremendous challenge. Continuously growing a partnership with your spouse and raising a family is equally daunting. Somehow you have to get both done. It is a situation of and/and, not either/or.

When I was up and coming in product management at General Foods, I had a family with three young boys at home. My commute back and forth to the company was exactly 22 minutes. For years, I left work precisely at the time that would allow me to drive home and walk in the door just as our family dinner was being served. Missing this moment was a rare occasion indeed. Other people hung around the office later into the evening. I chose to take work home, but I only got to it after the family finished dinner and the boys were doing their homework.

Years later, at a large event marking 60th birthdays for Sarah and me, our three sons gave a short tribute to our family and our parenting, including humorous stories and memories of growing up in our household. One of them remarked that his most cherished memory was that his Dad made it home every night for family dinner.

It made me feel I had struck the right balance.

The balance you strike will likely be different than it was for me. Regardless, balance is an imperative for a successful career and a happy family.

BOB'S WISDOM: Striking the right balance between work and your personal life makes you a high performer in your career.

Staying Calm, Cool, and Collected

I have found that two of the most important essentials for surviving in business and in life are a metaphorical bulletproof vest and a waterproof back. You need these when seriously stressful moments or circumstances begin to plague you, and extra tenacity and endurance are required to see things through.

Put on the bulletproof vest when you are taking onboard direct shots from the media, regulators, competitors, or even from your partners or boss. Listen to the just ones, but use the vest to repel the unjust ones. Take in comments that are well-informed and appropriate, and use the bulletproof vest to deflect those that are not. The vest helps you keep calm and not overreact, which is a fatal mistake in times of stress, especially in the international business world.

The bulletproof vest served me well in the year after I joined Cordiant as Chief Executive. It seemed that no matter how well we performed, every article in the trade press would start off with the line "The beleaguered Cordiant PLC" and then go on to rehash the departure of the Saatchi brothers a year earlier. In reality, business was significantly improving but it was some time before we could break the syndrome of negative lead-ins. My bulletproof vest kept me strong.

The waterproof back is most handy for those times when you are part of a broader group being criticized, but the commentary does not apply specifically to you. You will likely have to sit and listen to it, but maintain your cool, and just let it roll like water off a duck's back.

BOB'S WISDOM: Develop a bulletproof vest and a waterproof back and don't overreact to criticism or stress.

A Formula for Success

My career has been built around a consumer point of view. The first 28 years in business were spent in consumer packaged goods, and the last 14 in the advertising industry. While we develop advertising for technologically complex companies such as Toyota, we do not have to build the car, we just have to know what people want to drive and how to sell it to them.

Accordingly, my formula for success has been "one part brains, two parts common sense." When the formula is reversed, it usually leads to overthinking and undue analysis that invariably produce unsuccessful initiatives.

This formula was instilled in me by my initial brand assignment—when the three-inch thick binder filled with facts and figures on START Instant Breakfast Drink did not save us from the common sense fact that our market was being inundated with a bumper crop of low-cost natural orange juice.

Perhaps it was another experience at the sophisticated General Foods Corporation where our incredible technical ability enabled us to develop a soybean-based healthy alternative to bacon which was overwhelmed by the common sense facts that it looked like "facon" and tasted like cardboard. No amount of cholesterol reduction could have sold that product, yet the company worked on it for years.

An additional complement to common sense is street smarts. This is the practical stuff that you do not learn at Harvard College or Harvard Business School. Rather, you pick it up out in the real world via the school of hard knocks.

There has been a lot of analysis as to why the first President Bush lost his re-election campaign to Bill Clinton. How could the hero of

Desert Storm lose to an upstart governor from Arkansas? Political pun-dits often attribute his defeat to the fact that he raised taxes.

For me, something entirely different told me he would lose. It was the day he was filmed in a supermarket and seemed dumbfounded by the presence of a scanner that had been in routine use for years. This is the moment when the American public saw that he was divorced from the real world, common sense, and street smarts.

BOB'S WISDOM: One part brains and two parts common sense is the right formula for success in a consumer business.

Listen to Your Barber

I was living in Greensboro, North Carolina, as the first President Bush was wrapping up Desert Storm. Saddam Hussein had been driven from Kuwait, but Bush and his advisors decided not to go all the way to Baghdad and remove his government. I remarked on this to my barber, who was Lebanese. He said, "Oh, of course not. It is official U.S. policy to keep Saddam in power. That way, the Saudis will continue to be scared of him and permit you to have bases in their country." I can remember thinking at the time, "Hey, he may be right."

If you want to find out what is going on in the real world, talk to the guy who is driving your taxi around New York City. Do not just shuffle papers in the backseat—you can do that later. Take advantage of the opportunity to understand the input and the thinking of someone with whom you would not normally have a chance to communicate. While living in London, I learned the most about life in England from the company drivers—Arthur, Lofty, Ray, and Tom.

When I was in the coffee business and spent a lot of time on planes, I used to ask the person sitting next to me, "What is the best cup of coffee that you've had in the last two weeks?" People rarely mentioned a brand or a type of coffee. Rather, they invariably brought up a coffee-drinking occasion. This reinforced my understanding of the importance of the social side of coffee and helped explain why people would pay several dollars for a cup when being served in a retail establishment, but switch brands in the supermarket for a price difference of ten cents per can.

Similarly, my wife Sarah's explanations of how and why she made choices between competitive brands were of great benefit to me and subsequently to the company (and she sometimes went for the competing brands!).

BOB'S WISDOM: Get out and live life as a consumer. Talk up your business and expose yourself to the diversity of society.

Two Words You Should Avoid

In business, reality is subject to ever-changing variables. The assumptions you make at one moment in time are not likely to be relevant or appropriate the next time around. "Never" and "Always" are two words that often start you off on the wrong foot, and you should studiously avoid using them.

Consider this. When I was growing up, there were three barriers in track and field that people said would never be broken. They were the four-minute mile, the seven-foot high jump, and the fifteen-foot pole vault. Today, dramatically exceeding those performance levels is routine. Even high school milers can now run the mile below four minutes. The people who used the word "never" about the high jump and pole vault failed to envision the "Fosbury Flop" or the use of fiberglass poles. Innovation frequently changes the status quo.

When professional players were sanctioned in the Olympic Games, the United States put together the basketball "Dream Team" using NBA players headlined by Michael Jordan. After their dramatic first performance, sportscasters were saying the United States thereafter would "always" win gold. However, for many years thereafter, similar NBA-fed U.S. basketball teams fared poorly in international competition and were barely in contention. The "Redeem Team" finally got back on track at the 2008 Beijing Olympics. It remains to be seen what will happen in future years.

On a more mundane level, when I went to work in the Maxwell House Coffee Division at General Foods, the litany was that packing instant coffee in a glass carafe that could be heated was always sure to be a winner. For a while it was, until the day when everybody already had one, and the next promotion sat around retail stores for weeks.

BOB'S WISDOM: "Always" and "Never" are dangerous words when having to make assumptions.

Have Fun While You Work

One of my most satisfying and rewarding personal philosophies has been to "have fun while you work." In fact, I included this in the Personal Statement I wrote after attending the Aspen Institute, and it has been an ongoing part of my executive style.

There are several reasons this "have fun while you work" philosophy is important to me. The first is that it has made the daily challenges of work a lot more enjoyable. It keeps me upbeat and optimistic as a person. I can honestly say that I have never had a day when I did not look forward to going to work.

The second reason is that this philosophy has helped to make me more productive and successful in my career because of the positive effect it has on all the people who work together with me. If people enjoy working in your organization and being with you in meetings and planning sessions, they will be all the more motivated to work hard and contribute generously.

When I was in product management, it was a job that had "responsibility without authority." I could not tell my supportive functional colleagues how to spend their time and what to do. Rather, I had to motivate them, and earn what I called my "disproportionate fair share" of their time on my business initiatives. I was successful because I created an environment in which people enjoyed working with me on my brands.

To have fun, you do not have to be a joke teller. However, sometimes you have to make the effort to keep things light. A big part of this is your tone of voice and how you say things. It also helps to be willing to poke fun at yourself, or say things that consciously seek to level the status in the room.

You should aspire to be a person that people look forward to collaborating with no matter how tough the challenges. It is also a good idea to learn how to tell stories and illustrate complex issues with analogies that everyone can relate to.

Being happy in my work has helped me stay at the top of my game while enjoying every day. And being happy is a great antidote to executive burnout.

BOB'S WISDOM: If you stay happy in your work, you and your team will be more productive and successful day-to-day and over the long term.

Foster a Foreign Language,
It Makes You Less Foreign

When I was in high school, I studied French for three years. My teacher was Madame Jean Low. She had been born in France, and despite many years of living in the United States, she remained extremely proud of her French heritage. We learned proper pronunciation and sang songs like the French national anthem, *La Marseillaise*, or French childhood songs like *Sur le pont d'Avignon*. Madame Low was a wonderful teacher, and when I applied to college, I thought I might major in French. That is, before I became enamored of economics.

As President and CEO of General Foods Worldwide Coffee and International Foods, I began to travel the world. I had not really used my knowledge of French up to that point, but suddenly it started to become useful in a number of countries, so I undertook a refresher course with Berlitz tapes.

As I began to interact with executives from other countries, I found that most of them were bilingual. In countries like Switzerland, it is common to find executives who speak at least four languages. In a world where much of business is now global in its scope, these executives have an edge. Not only in speaking multiple languages, but with the multicultural understanding that accompanies such a capability.

Historically, most American businesspeople are less fluent with languages and therefore less attuned to cultural differences. One reason for this is that many countries in the world seem to be using English as the universal language of business, so some Americans easily—and wrongly—conclude, "Why bother?"

When we merged Saatchi & Saatchi PLC into Publicis Groupe in the year 2000, I became a member of their Conseil de Surveillance, the French Board. Publicis previously had an alliance with Foote, Cone &

Belding Advertising of Chicago and it had not been a happy relationship because the Midwest culture from the United States had not blended very well with the French culture and heritage.

New to the Conseil, I was determined to change this. The Board meetings were all conducted in French, albeit simultaneous translation was available. While I would have to avail myself of that capability for business purposes, I decided that I would make my introductory remarks to the Board in French, both as a gesture of respect and as a sign that I had no intention of being an "Ugly American." I wrote my remarks in English, translated them into French and practiced my delivery in advance.

My introductory remarks were very well received, and indeed, taken as a sign that this new relationship would be a very positive one. Madame Jean Low would have been proud!

Today, Publicis Groupe prides itself on being a multicultural company and its motto is "Viva La Difference." Viva in Spanish, La in French, and Difference in English.

BOB'S WISDOM: Cultivating a foreign language is a necessary skill; make sure you accompany it with an appreciation for multiple cultures.

Plus ça Change, Plus c'est la Même Chose

"Plus ça change, plus c'est la même chose" means "The more things change, the more they stay the same." This enduring French expression is the reason you should want to build a dossier of your own wisdom.

As I write this, I have been associated with Saatchi & Saatchi in one way or another for 14 years—an eternity in the advertising industry. We currently have 16 people on our Worldwide Executive Board, and there are only three of us who have been there a decade or more.

It would be difficult for me to tell you how many times we revisit the same subjects in the light of a current day's circumstances—how to handle a client situation or how to strike the right balance between revenue, costs, and profit. All I can say is that it has been many, many times.

It is not that we are stupid. It is just that in an ever-faster moving world, the circumstances and therefore the tactics must keep changing—but rarely do the underlying principles change. Based on what I have learned from my own experiences, human nature and basic business practices do not really shift very much over the years. The notion that "I have been to this party before" gives you a good foundation for dealing with most issues.

As you go forward, the ability to come at things from the vantage point of values, beliefs, and principles, combined with soundness of judgment honed by experience and exposure (wisdom) is a good place to start.

BOB'S WISDOM: Accumulate your own set of "wisdoms" to keep you principled in an ever-changing world.

Be True to Yourself

When I was thinking of where to apply to college, my guidance counselor said the thought of applying to Harvard College was ridiculous, but my mother said, "We'll take a flyer on it."

When I was thinking about whether to take the job as Chief Executive at Cordiant, one of my advisors said, "Don't touch it with a 10-foot pole," but I thought it would be an adventure in life.

When the idea of writing a book crystallized for me, and with these two situations in mind, I once again sought advice. I called two friends who had written books to help determine whether this was something I should undertake.

The first person said, "Don't do it!" He indicated that you had to start by writing a proposal and then submit it to a literary agent to sell the idea of the book. In my case, he thought it was unlikely they would buy it for two reasons. First, to write a great book, you had to be a great writer, and he was unsure that I could meet that test. Second, he felt that to sell a business book, you already had to be famous, like a Jack Welch or Lou Gerstner, and while I was accomplished, I was not famous.

I thanked him for his input and then called my second advisor, Kevin Roberts, the primary recipient of my advice, counsel, and perspective over the past 12 years. Kevin thought that writing this book was a great idea. He felt I had accumulated a lot of wisdom over the years, and that people would be interested in learning from it. He also felt that the process of getting it done would be personally exhilarating and deeply satisfying for me.

Indeed, it has been an energizing process to compile this collection of my life's stories and the wisdom I've gained. They represent the experiences, strategies, and tactics in business and in my life that have worked for me. You will decide which of them might be helpful to you now and into the future.

Here the story has a bit of a twist. When I finished writing this book, I did indeed seek out a literary agent who could garner the support that would optimize its chances for success. Knowing who you are, what you want, and being open-minded and receptive to change are essential to success in life.

Accordingly, this leads to my final piece of wisdom for you, which is "Be True to Yourself."

You are a unique person and in the final analysis, after all this input, you alone must decide what is right for you. Nobody else can do that for you. Nor should you want them to. The rewards in life and in business are simply greater when you are true to yourself.

BOB'S WISDOM: Be true to yourself, do it happily, and be prepared to live with the outcomes.

Acknowledgments

When I decided to write this book, I was naive as to the complexities I would face. Kevin Roberts provided encouragement and told me, "Contact Brian Sweeney."

Brian Sweeney is the Chairman of SweeneyVesty, a strategic communications company; and simply put, without Brian and his team there would be no book. They had detailed knowledge about how to proceed, starting with a blank piece of paper all the way through to the finished project. They have my enduring gratitude.

A special vote of thanks goes to Kubé Jones-Neill, who immediately understood my voice, and helped polish and finalize the text.

A number of people at Saatchi & Saatchi provided both inspiration and suggestions, including Kevin Roberts, Bob Isherwood, Richard Hytner, Richard Myers, and Roger Kennedy.

My wife, Sarah and our three sons, Perry, John, and Stephen all provided support and encouragement, and they tolerated the seemingly endless periods of drafting and rewriting.

Steve Hanselman at Level 5 Media became my literary agent and was enormously helpful in getting us to a great publisher.

The team at John Wiley, including Matt Holt, Richard Narramore, Peter Knapp, and Kim Dayman then did an excellent job of bringing the book to the marketplace.

Finally, there are numerous people mentioned throughout the text who contributed to my career and my potential to accumulate wisdom. Without them, there would not have been anything to write about.

Index